Leckie×Leckie

Scotland's leading educational publishers

Help your child with
English

Makes English Easy!

Susan Dodds

Contents

Contents

How to get the most from this book

Help Your Child with English is written for you and your child to work through together at home to grow your child's ability in English. It's the perfect solution for all parents wanting to make certain that their children are completely up to speed with this important subject. With clear guidance to help children of all abilities practise and learn, **Help Your Child with English** has masses of creative activities to make learning English fun, even for the most restless child.

Check-up tasks are provided to help you assess how well your child has understood each topic.

What this book contains

Help Your Child with English is closely aligned to Scotland's **Curriculum for Excellence** to make certain that your child is learning exactly the right English at the right time. It covers all English topics included in **Level 2** of the curriculum, routinely studied by children between the ages of 9 and 12, though sometimes by younger or older learners. Children studying at KS2 will also find this a useful resource. **Help Your Child with English** will provide invaluable assistance for children during the transition from primary to secondary school – when some can struggle to keep up with English.

Parents are naturally concerned that their children's work is legible, correctly spelled and accurately punctuated. These elements are all important; however, possessing the skills of good listening and talking and being able to read and write for both pleasure and a purpose are equally important.

Make learning fun

Every topic of **Help Your Child with English** is packed full of fun activities. Designed to help embed your child's understanding of English, the activities are highly creative, providing many varied opportunities to practise English.

Whether you want to help with homework or build on what your child is learning in class, **Help Your Child with English** covers all the core subjects. This simple step-by-step approach makes certain that learning isn't a chore for your child and that learning English becomes that little bit easier.

Top Tips for Parents

- Find a quiet, comfortable place to work, away from distractions.
- Ask what English your child is doing at school and choose an appropriate topic.
- Tackle one topic at a time.
- Help with reading where necessary, and ensure your child understands what to do.
- Help and encourage your child to check his or her own answers as each activity is completed.
- Discuss with your child what he or she has learned.
- Let your child return to his or her favourite pages once they have been completed, to play the games and talk about the activities with you or a partner.
- Reward your child with plenty of praise and encouragement.

The book's activities encourage your child to practise English, often with a friend or an adult. Working in pairs on activities is a great approach not only to learning through talking about English but also to retain interest. The activities are both challenging and creative, and have clear links to real-life situations, showing how much English matters all around us in our environment.

Children can begin to assess how well they are doing in each area by using the 'traffic light' boxes in the **High 5!** features. They should decide whether they 'need help' (by ticking the red box), 'think I'm there' (by ticking the yellow box) or 'I've got it!' (by ticking the green box).

Check-up tasks

Help!   Keep going!   Good to go!

Check-up tasks are provided to help you assess how well your child has understood each topic. Use the coloured 'traffic lights' to assess how well your child is doing in each area, and whether more practice might be needed.

○ ○ ○

Keep a diary

This section will show you:

- why diaries are used
- how to keep a personal diary in order to record your thoughts and feelings as well as any significant events in your life.

Top Tips for Parents

- If your child doesn't already have one, a copy of Anne Frank's Diary would be ideal. Encourage your child to read at least parts of it before starting on their own diary. It will give them ideas as to what they could write and how effective a way it is to unburden their private thoughts and feelings.
- Assure your child that you will not intrude into their privacy by reading their diary.

What are diaries?

Diaries are used for two purposes.

1   As a handy reminder of things you need to do, places to go, people you have to meet and times for doing things. These diaries usually last for a year: a new diary needs to be bought when the old one runs out. There are desk diaries, small pocket or handbag diaries and electronic diaries. Some mobile phones can be used as diaries. Calendars are often used in the same way as these diaries, with appointments being written on them in the same way as appointments would be written in diaries. You may have a calendar like this on your wall at home. Most appointment diaries are discarded soon after they are replaced by new ones.

2   As a way of recording all the important and interesting events that happen in a person's life. Diaries like these are written up after the events have happened, not before like an appointment diary. These diaries are extremely personal and are often kept very private. The writers may record personal feelings and thoughts they would rather no one else read. Many celebrities who publish their autobiographies use their diaries to remind them of events and people they wish to write about. Without their diaries they may forget names, events, thoughts and dates. It is not necessary to write a diary like this every day. Items should be added only when you feel there is something important or memorable to write about.

A very famous diary was written during the Second World War (1939–45) by a young Dutch girl called Anne Frank. Anne was a Jew. Jews were being persecuted at this time by the Nazis, with millions of them being sent to concentration camps. Anne, along with her family and some friends, was hidden in a secret room above an office. Kind friends brought food and drink for them. To while away the hours of silence and inactivity, Anne wrote a diary, which revealed her thoughts and described events. Anne referred to her diary as 'Kitty'. Each entry begins with the day and date it was written. The names of some people were changed to save them from being identified. Anne's hiding place was eventually found by the Nazis and she was taken to a concentration camp where she died, but her diary was saved and later published. It has since been read by millions of people around the world. You may like to get a copy of the book to read yourself. Read the following extract:

> **Thursday, 16 March 1944**
> Dearest Kitty,
>   The weather is gorgeous, indescribably beautiful; I'll be going up to the attic in a moment.
>   I now know why I'm so much more restless than Peter. He has his own room, where he can work, dream, think and sleep. I'm constantly being chased from one corner to another. I'm never alone in the room I share with Dussel, though I long to be so much. That's another reason why I take refuge in the attic. When I'm there, or with you, I can be myself, at least for a little while. Still, I don't want to whinge. On the contrary, I want to be brave!

The Diary of a Young Girl, Anne Frank, Puffin, 2007

Go and do!

Keep your own diary whilst working on this book. Write down all the things that happen to you that you feel are important – bad as well as good. Mention the people you meet, places you go to, things that happen, your feelings and thoughts. It is not necessary to use a proper diary. A special notebook would be ideal. Remember to write the date above each entry. You could also give your diary a name as Anne Frank did. You may enjoy this task so much that you continue to keep a diary for the rest of your life!

High 5!

- I have regularly made entries in my personal diary.

- I recorded the day and date before each diary entry.

- I chose to write about a variety of events and feelings in my diary.

Check-up tasks

Help!   Keep going!   Good to go!

Diaries are very personal things. It would be advisable to ask permission from your child before reading the diary and to respect his or her wishes about this. You could simply talk together about the diary. Did he or she enjoy keeping it and why? Does he or she intend to continue writing it, etc?

Nouns, pronouns and adjectives

This section will explain to you:

- what nouns, pronouns and adjectives are
- the difference between a common noun, a proper noun and a collective noun
- how to use adjectives to enhance your writing.

Top Tips for Parents

- Once your child understands what nouns and adjectives are, refer to them as such all the time.
- If your child is unsure whether a word is a noun, etc, encourage him or her to look it up in a dictionary.

Nouns

Nouns are often called naming words. They are the names of:

- **people**   boy, Colin, mother, etc.
- **animals**   cat, hyena, elephant, etc.
- **places**   Scotland, Glasgow, countryside, etc.
- **objects**   desk, pencil, car, etc.
- **events**   gala, Christmas, party, etc.
- **feelings** sadness, weakness, fear, etc.

Proper nouns are always written with a capital letter at the start of the word. They are individual names.

Common nouns require capital letters only if they are at the start of a sentence.
We asked John to send us a postcard of the Eiffel Tower from Paris.
John, Eiffel Tower and *Paris* are proper nouns, while *postcard* is a common noun.

Collective nouns refer to a group of nouns.
a herd of cattle   *a flock of birds*   *a pack of wolves*
Herd, flock and *pack* are collective nouns.

Pronouns

Pronouns are words used in place of nouns.
Dad said he wouldn't be able to meet his son after school as the car had a flat tyre. It was in the garage being fixed.
He, his and *it* are pronouns. Other pronouns include: *she, her, they, we, us, our, them*

Adjectives

Adjectives are words that describe nouns. They give us more information.

The old man, wearing a blue coat, staggered along the dusty road.

Old, *blue* and *dusty* give us more information about the man, his coat and the road.

Exercises

Underline the <u>nouns</u> in the following sentences with one colour and the adjectives with a different colour.

1 The small <u>boy</u> fell off his red <u>bicycle</u> and scuffed his new <u>trainers</u>.

2 Skipping along the country <u>path</u>, <u>Amy</u> saw an unusual <u>flock</u> of green <u>birds</u> in the tall <u>trees</u>.

3 The delighted <u>children</u> went sledging in the snowy <u>weather</u>.

4 A large <u>swarm</u> of <u>bees</u> gathered noisily beside the <u>hive</u> in the <u>cornfield</u>.

Go and do!

1 Look through a book you enjoy reading. When you come across any unusual nouns or adjectives add them to lists of such words. Try to find nouns and adjectives you wouldn't normally use in your writing. Can you find fifteen of each?

Now use a dictionary to check if you chose well. Were they all nouns and adjectives? Have another go if you made some mistakes.

High 5!

• I know what nouns and pronouns are and can recognise them in both oral and written work. ☐ ☐ ☐

• I understand the differences between a common noun, a proper noun, a collective noun and a pronoun. ☐ ☐ ☐

Check-up tasks

Help!   Keep going!   Good to go!

Ask your child to point out the common nouns, proper nouns, collective nouns, pronouns and adjectives from the following:

mutter mountain Jupiter run happy flock Spain it shoes
weariness bicycle apple happiness they attractive silliness
Alan fantastic crawl sensible spider interesting black portrait
Glasgow pack Easter my

○   ○   ○

Verbs and adverbs

This section will explain to you:

- what verbs and adverbs are
- the differences between the past, present and future tenses
- how adverbs can be used to add more information and detail to your writing.

Top Tips for Parents

- If your child is unsure if a word is a verb or an adverb, encourage him or her to look it up in the dictionary.
- The internet is a great tool if further practice on verbs or adverbs is required. Simply type 'adverbs' into a search engine before clicking 'enter'. A good interactive site is:
  www.bbc.co.uk/ skillswise/ words/ grammar/ interestsentences/ adverbs/

Verbs

Verbs are often called 'doing words'. They can be:

- past tense – happened earlier, e.g. yesterday or last week.
- present tense – happening now.
- future tense – not yet happened.

Roy <u>kicked</u> his ball across the field. – Past tense
Roy <u>is kicking</u> his ball across the field. – Present tense
Roy <u>will kick</u> his ball across the field. – Future tense

It is important to remember when writing not to change the verb tense, e.g. do not start writing in the past tense, switch to present tense and then back to the past tense.

Sally went slowly into the classroom. She looked around the room. Her gaze fell on Samantha. 'Good,' she thought, 'now for some fun.'

Sally is bullying Samantha. Samantha is scared of her.

Notice how the first part of the passage was written in the past tense but changed to present tense in the last sentence. You can see that *went, looked, fell* and *thought* are past tense but *is* implies it is happening now. This is present tense.

Adverbs

Adverbs are words that give more information about verbs. They tell us how, where, why or when something was done. Many adverbs end in 'ly', although not all words ending in 'ly' are adverbs.

- *Claire walked <u>miserably</u> to school.*
- *<u>Tomorrow</u> Ian will walk to school.*

Adverbs do not always need to be beside the verb they are referring to and can occur at the beginning or end of a sentence.

- Sukjit swam _lazily_ across the pool.
- _Lazily,_ Sukjit swam across the pool.
- Sukjit swam across the pool _lazily._

 ## Go and do!

1 Look through an old comic or magazine. Cut out any interesting verbs or adverbs you think you could use in your writing. (Remember to ask first if the magazine is not your own.) Now write a short paragraph, on any subject, using as many of these words as you can. Remember to vary the position of the adverbs in the sentence. Starting some sentences with adverbs can make your writing much more interesting.

2 What are you interested in? Using a reference book, the internet or newspapers, collect verbs which are specific to your interest. For example, if you are interested in swimming you may choose 'dive', 'crawl' or 'breathe'. Make a table listing your interests and as many verbs associated with them as you can find. Check in a dictionary that the words you have chosen are indeed verbs.

3 Look at the verbs you have listed. Can you pair each one up with a really good adverb?

 ## High 5!

- I understand what a verb is and what an adverb is.

- I can recognise verbs and adverbs in both oral and written work.

- I can use adverbs to add greater detail to my writing.

Check-up tasks

Help! Keep going! Good to go!

Ask your child to alter, either in writing or orally, the following sentences by changing only the verbs and adverbs.

- Slowly the train chugged up the steep hill.
- Sue changed her library book yesterday.
- The dog happily buried his bone in the garden.
- The teacher spoke angrily to the class.
- We crossed the busy road cautiously.

Dictionaries

This section will:

- help you understand the layout and content of dictionaries
- explain how to use 'lead words' when searching for a word in dictionaries
- explain what a 'root' word is.

What is a dictionary?

A dictionary is a book of words arranged in alphabetical order. Amongst other information, words listed will often give the definition of the words (there is often more than one meaning), how the words should be pronounced, their parts of speech, the words in their plural forms, their origin and other words derived from them.

Collins Online English Dictionary definition (meaning) of:

listen
VERB

1. to concentrate on hearing something,
2. to take heed; pay attention, I told you many times but you wouldn't listen,

Old English *hlysnan*; related to Old High German *lūstrēn*

◇ **listener NOUN**

To help us find words, dictionaries also have the first word on a double page at the top of the left-hand page and the final word of the second page at the top of the right-hand page. These are called 'lead' or 'head' words. All words which fall alphabetically between these words can be found on these two pages.

Often words do not appear as separate entries but alongside their 'root' or 'guide' words. For example, in the above example the noun 'listener' appears under the definition of the root word 'listen'.

Top Tips for Parents

- By the time children are in their last year of primary school they should be able to use an adult dictionary with ease. However, if you have access only to a child's dictionary this will do. Be aware, though, that many words will not appear in these easier dictionaries.
- Collins Dictionary is available as a book (in both child and adult versions), a pocket edition, an electronic version and online.
- Youngsters will often say a word is not in the dictionary. Remind them they must very often look for the root word first. Don't give in to temptation and point the word out. If necessary say, 'The word you're looking for is on this page', and wait for them to find it themselves.

Exercises

Many dictionaries give lists of information on other topics before and after the main definition section. These can include abbreviations, capital cities, Roman numerals and weight conversions.

- Look at your dictionary. Write down the titles of some of the different lists of information in the dictionary which you may find useful.

- Write the following words in alphabetical order. Which of them might you find on dictionary pages with the lead words 'tarmac – team'?

task   temper   tarnish   taste   target   tape   tartan   team   tear

 # Go and do!

- Take some tins and packets from the kitchen cupboard. Arrange them in alphabetical order along the table or worktop.

- Read the labels on the alphabetically arranged items from the kitchen cupboard. Note down any abbreviations you find. On a piece of paper draw three columns with headings 'Abbreviation', 'My guess' and 'Meaning'.

  Write each abbreviation in the first column, what you think it means in the second column, then check it in your dictionary and write the correct meaning in the third column. How accurate were your guesses?

 # High 5!

- I can use the dictionary to tell me not just the definition of words but other information as well. ☐ ☐ ☐

- I regularly use a dictionary to make sure I understand what I am reading. ☐ ☐ ☐

- I can use 'lead' words to help me quickly find what I'm looking for in the dictionary. ☐ ☐ ☐

- I know to search for the 'root' word when looking for a word in the dictionary. ☐ ☐ ☐

Check-up tasks

Help!   Keep going!   Good to go!

Hand your child a dictionary and ask him or her to carry out the following task.

Find the following words and read out their dictionary definitions.

notched   copse   subdued

◯   ◯   ◯

Thesauri

This section will:

- explain what thesauri are and the correct way to use them
- show links between how you use a thesaurus and how you use a dictionary
- demonstrate the value of using a thesaurus when searching for more powerful words to use in your writing.

Top Tips for Parents

- As with dictionaries, your child should now be able to use an adult thesaurus. However, if all that is available is a school or children's thesaurus this will be fine, although the range of words will be less extensive than in an adult version.
- Thesauri can be bought from all good booksellers or on the internet. As well as standard versions, Collins publishes pocket, electronic and online versions.

What is a thesaurus?

A thesaurus (plural: thesauri) is a book that lists words alongside other words with similar meanings. A thesaurus, therefore, is a book of synonyms. As with dictionaries, to help you find the word you are looking for quickly, there are lead words at the top of each page which give the first word on the left-hand page and the final word on the right-hand page.

Using a thesaurus when writing an imaginative story, letter, report, etc. will improve your range of vocabulary, which in turn will raise the standard of your finished work.

- You must remember, though, if you choose an alternative word from a thesaurus, to make sure you are using it in the correct way.

Subtract
– deduct, remove, dock, diminish

Although all these words mean 'to make smaller', there are subtle differences in their meaning when used in sentences.

If you subtract eight from ten, you get two.

We could replace *subtract* with *deduct* and the meaning would not alter.

If you deduct eight from ten, you get two.

If we replace *subtract* with *diminish*, however, then the sentence makes no sense. You cannot diminish eight from ten!

- Some words may be used as a verb or a noun, etc. so again be careful which alternative word you choose. Replace a noun with a noun and an adjective with an adjective.

> **Flood**
> – swamp, deluge, spate, inundate

Swamp and *inundate* are verbs. *Deluge* and *spate* are nouns.

The flood covered the fields.

In this sentence *flood* is a noun. Instead of *flood* we could use *deluge* or *spate*. Either would make sense in the sentence.

The overflowing river began to flood the field.

Now *flood* is a verb. This time we would need to choose *inundate* or *swamp* as possible alternatives.

 ## Go and do!

- Create your own word search. Look in your thesaurus and choose a word that has many synonyms or choose one from the list below.

walk	saw	happy	teach	lift	tired

Make a list of alternative words for the word you choose, then use the following website or squared paper to make a super word search.

puzzlemaker.discoveryeducation.com/WordSearchSetupForm.asp

 ## High 5!

- I understand that a thesaurus is a book of synonyms.

- I realise that I use a thesaurus in a similar way to how I use a dictionary.

- I can use a thesaurus to improve my choice of words when writing stories, reports, etc.

Check-up tasks

Help!   Keep going!   Good to go!

Ask your child to use a thesaurus to find suitable synonyms for the underlined words.

1   We will <u>travel</u> to India this summer.

2   It was hard <u>work</u> digging the garden.

3   I was <u>confused</u> by all the choices I was given.

Spelling

> ## This section will:
>
> - explain why there are many words in the English language with unusual spellings
> - give tips on ways you can improve your spelling
> - link spelling to the section on the dictionary (pages 12–13).

Why bother with correct spelling?

Spelling is important. For some people learning and remembering spelling is easy. For others, spelling is a challenge. They find learning and remembering spelling difficult and cannot always see when words are incorrectly spelled. If you fall into this last category, don't worry. There are many ways to help you learn spelling. The important thing is not to give up. Keep trying until you find a method that suits you.

English is a difficult language to learn and write due to its multicultural past. Our island has been invaded by many different countries and peoples over thousands of years. Each invader brought its own language. Words and phrases from these languages, which include spelling, have all come together to create the English we now speak.

Homonyms

These are words that are spelled differently and have different meanings but sound the same, e.g. ate, eight.

Silent letters

Many words contain letters that we do not pronounce but must be included when spelling the word. These are made more tricky because, depending on where we live and on our accent, what is perhaps a silent letter in one part of the country is not a silent letter in others.

lamb   *thumb*   *yolk*   *talk*   *write*

Top Tips for Parents

- Encourage your child to use a dictionary to check for correct spelling and remind him or her to use the spellcheck facilities on some computer programs.
- Investing in an electronic spellchecker is worthwhile, especially if your child has specific spelling difficulties. Collins' Spellchecker is very reasonably priced and can be bought from good internet sites such as Amazon. Alternatively there are many good online spellchecker sites.
- Many schools now teach spelling through **active spelling** activities such as blue vowels, bubble writing, syllables and pyramid writing. If you're unsure what techniques your child has been taught, talk to your child or his/her teacher.
- If you are using internet spelling sites with your child, try to ensure they are British sites, to avoid confusion between English and American spelling.

Compound words

Compound words are words made from two or more other words.

somewhere   however   ladybird   tablecloth

 Exercises

ough

The four letters *ough* appear in many words but can have four different sounds. Draw a grid like the one below. Place each word in the box below in the correct column.

> trough   bough   rough   cough   enough   though   dough   rough

Ough Pronounced 'uff'	Ough Pronounced 'ow'	Ough Pronounced 'off'	Ough Pronounced 'o'

Go and do!

Log on to the following website; you'll find lots of great games to help you learn spelling. Have fun!

www.woodlands-junior.kent.sch.uk/interactive/literacy.html

High 5!

- I understand that many English words have unusual spellings. ☐ ☐ ☐

- I regularly practise spelling the words I find difficult. ☐ ☐ ☐

- I can use active spelling techniques and fun games on the internet to help make learning spelling fun. ☐ ☐ ☐

- I self-correct spelling using a dictionary or spellchecker. ☐ ☐ ☐

Check-up tasks

Help!   Keep going!   Good to go!

Using the *'look, say, cover, write, check'* method * and/or an active spelling technique, ask your child to learn any words you feel he or she may find difficult.

*See page 96.

Apostrophes

This section will:

- explain when and how you should use apostrophes.

Top Tips for Parents

- A common mistake made by children is to add an apostrophe to every word that ends with 's'. Watch out for this and, if your child should make this error, point it out and ask him or her to correct it.
- Try the following sites for extra help and games with apostrophes. primaryhomeworkhelp.co.uk/interactive/literacy2.htm#apo

www.bbc.co.uk/skillswise/words/grammar/punctuation/apostrophes/

When do you use apostrophes?

Apostrophes are used on two important occasions.

1 **To indicate ownership.**

Look at the following examples.

- An apostrophe is used to show that something belongs to someone or something.

    The boy's ball rolled onto the busy road.

    The apostrophe is used to show that the ball belongs to the boy. If we did not use the apostrophe we would need to say:

    The ball belonging to the boy rolled onto the busy road.

- When the possessive noun (this means the word or noun that something belongs to) is plural, then the apostrophe is placed after the 's'.

    The dogs' leads are hanging on the hook.

    The apostrophe is after the 's' so we know that the leads belong to more than one dog.

- If the noun is plural but doesn't end in an 's', then we add the apostrophe and 's':

    The women's shoes were lined up against the wall.

    The shoes belonging to the women were lined up against the wall.

If you're not sure which word should take the apostrophe or whether it is singular or plural, reword the sentence in your head or out loud using the words 'belonging to'. Look at how the explanations above have been worded.

2   To indicate that a letter or letters have been missed out.

He is – *he's*   They will – *they'll*   Of the clock – *o'clock*

We have – *we've*   I should not – *I shouldn't*

Remember

Remember, you should **not** use apostrophes when the word is simply
a plural with an 's' at the end.
I picked the apples from the tree.

Exercises

Tick the correctly punctuated sentences.

1   Jim's hat blew off in the breeze. ☐   2   The teacher marked the children's work. ☐

3   The girl's books were in their bags. ☐   4   Pauls friends' are coming to his party. ☐

5   Amanda's bike was stolen. ☐   6   The hamster's were in their cages. ☐

Write the following with apostrophes.

he would   they have   she is   it will   should not   can not

Go and do!

- Look through a favourite book or a newspaper. Find examples of apostrophe. Decide
  whether each shows **ownership** or **missing letters**. Write a list of at least five of each. For
  each, write out the longer, more formal, version.

High 5!

- I can use an apostrophe correctly to show ownership.   ☐ ☐ ☐

- When used to show ownership, I know when to place the apostrophe   ☐ ☐ ☐
  after the 's' to signify the word is plural.

- I can use an apostrophe correctly to show a letter, or letters, have been   ☐ ☐ ☐
  missed out.

Check-up tasks

Help!   Keep going!   Good to go!

Either copy a passage from a favourite book or write a short
paragraph yourself, missing out all the apostrophes. Ask your
child to go over it, replacing the missing punctuation. If he or
she uses a different coloured pencil or pen for the apostrophes,
this will make it easier to correct.

◯   ◯   ◯

Punctuation

This section will:

- explain why it is important to punctuate your writing correctly
- give examples of punctuation we should regularly use when writing
- show you when to use punctuation.

Top Tips for Parents

- Continually stress the importance of correct punctuation.
- Get a copy of the children's version of the book Eats, Shoots & Leaves: Why Commas Really Do Make a Difference!, by Lynne Truss, from a bookshop, online or from the library. This shows, in a fun and amusing way, how misinterpretations of a piece of text can arise through bad punctuation.

Is punctuation important?

Punctuation helps writing make sense. Without punctuation we would have difficulty reading stories, reports, letters, instructions, etc. Most punctuation is easy to understand and use but some punctuation requires a bit more concentration. Here we will look at the easier punctuation. You will find help on learning trickier punctuation, such as colons and semicolons, in other sections of this book.

Full stops

Full stops **are** used:

- at the end of sentences
- after abbreviations – *Prof., etc. e.g.*

Full stops are **not** used:

- after titles such as *Mr, Mrs, Dr*
- after capital letters which are abbreviations – *BBC, NATO*
- after abbreviations of measurement – *kg, cm*

Question marks

Question marks replace full stops at the end of sentences that ask questions.

Exclamation marks

Exclamation marks are used to show strong feeling. They are used to indicate fear, shouting, surprise, anger and happiness.

Speech marks

When writing dialogue use speech marks, sometimes called inverted commas, around the spoken words. All punctuation associated with the speech should also be inside the speech marks. See the section on Dialogue (pages 22–23).

Commas

Commas are used:

- **to separate items in a list** – *My salad consisted of lettuce, tomato, cheese, ham and peppers.*
- **to join two sentences together**. A connective must also be used – *I enjoy visiting Blackpool, however, I prefer going to London.* (See page 30 for more information on connectives.)
- **to isolate a phrase giving additional information** – *The dog, which was barking furiously, chased the man down the street.*

Parentheses (singular: parenthesis)

Parentheses are round or curved brackets. Parentheses are used in a similar way to commas that isolate phrases – *The Romans (and later the Vikings) invaded Britain more than a thousand years ago.*

Ellipsis

An ellipsis is three evenly spaced dots used to create suspense – *Ben walked purposefully over to Miranda. He slowly bent down and whispered in her ear before …*

 Go and do!

- Write each of the following on separate pieces of card.

• parentheses	• speech marks	• commas joining two
• question mark	• commas in a list	sentences together,
• exclamation mark	• commas isolating	using a connective
• full stop	a phrase	

Shuffle the cards and place them upside-down in a pile. Choose a topic, e.g. rivers, the supermarket, snow, the funfair. Turn over three of the cards. Write a paragraph about your chosen topic that incorporates the three types of punctuation you've turned over.

Check–up tasks

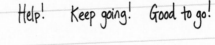 Help! Keep going! Good to go!

Play a game with your child. Choose a topic and challenge one another to write a sentence using punctuation of your choice. Place a time limit on the task. Award five points if the sentence, with correct punctuation, is written in under two minutes and three points if the correctly punctuated sentence takes longer than two minutes. Who has the most points after six sentences?

Dialogue

This section will:

- explain how to write dialogue successfully
- make links between writing dialogue and previous sections on adverbs (pages 10–11), the thesaurus (pages 14–15) and punctuation (pages 20–21).

previous sections on adverbs (pages 10–11), the thesaurus (pages 14–15) and punctuation (pages 20–21).

Top Tips for Parents

- When used in imaginative writing, dialogue does not need to be in standard English. Encourage your child to write just as the character would speak.

When to use dialogue

We use dialogue in imaginative writing to tell us more about what is happening in the story. If a character speaks in a particular dialect we can incorporate this into the speech.

A person from Glasgow might say: *'Pick that up for me hen.'*

However, a person from Yorkshire might say: *'Pick that up for me ducks.'*

The criteria for using dialogue in a piece of writing are:

- Always use a new line for each new speaker.
- Use correct punctuation, especially speech marks.
- Try to use more interesting words than 'said'.
- Describe how the characters speak using suitable adverbs.

Punctuation is very important when writing dialogue.

- Speech marks are always used around the words that are spoken.
  'I'm going to visit Gran,' stated Mum.
- Full stops, question marks, exclamation marks and commas that are part of spoken words should be included within the speech marks.
  'Why are you talking?' asked the teacher, *'You know this is a test.'*

 ## Exercises

Make a list of verbs you could use instead of 'said'. You can use a thesaurus.

Now make a list of adverbs that could be used with them, e.g. *roared – angrily, loudly.*

Put this list in a safe place to use later.

Punctuate the following sentences correctly.

1   the television's broken wailed the children

2   quick screamed everyone the tide's coming in

3   paul was fed up when are we going home he
    moaned

 ## Go and do!

- Divide a piece of A4 paper into four sections.
  - Imagine two friends have met in the park. What are they doing? What might they be talking about?
  - In each of the four sections of the storyboard draw a scene from the park with the two friends. Write the conversation they are having inside speech bubbles. Use your list of adverbs and synonyms for 'said' from earlier on to help you.
  - Now write out the scene. Remember to follow the criteria set out at the start of this section.

High 5!

When writing dialogue I have:

- used a new line for each new speaker   ☐ ☐ ☐

- used correct punctuation, especially speech marks   ☐ ☐ ☐

- used more interesting words than 'said'   ☐ ☐ ☐

- described how the characters speak, using suitable adverbs. ☐ ☐ ☐

Check-up tasks

Help!   Keep going!   Good to go!

Hand your child a short cartoon strip taken from a favourite comic. Ask him or her to replace speech bubbles with written dialogue. Give him or her a copy of the criteria required for dialogue and check that he or she is using it while writing.

◯   ◯   ◯

Colons

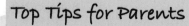

Top Tips for Parents

This section will:

- explain what a colon is and when you should use it.

- Using a colon in a list is easy for a child to understand. Don't worry if your child doesn't pick up the other use of a colon. Return to the subject every few months to help reinforce its use.
- Point out how the colon has been used on this and other pages.

What's the point of colons?

Colons are used when writing non-fiction or functional writing. Look at the instructions for assembling a toy or a piece of furniture. The list of components and each step of the instructions are often separated by colons and itemised by bullet points or numbers.

There are two uses for colons in writing.

1   **At the start of a list** – providing what comes before the colon makes sense if written on its own.

The pizza had all my favourite toppings: tomato, mushrooms, peppers and salami.
I love dogs: Golden Retrievers, Fox Terriers, Poodles, Greyhounds and German Shepherds.

Sometimes the list that follows the colon will be bullet-pointed:

Your task is to do the following:
- *Read page 26 of your textbook.*
- *Answer the questions at the bottom of the page.*
- *Hand the completed task to your teacher.*

On a camping holiday you need:
- *tent*
- *camping stove*
- *sleeping bag*
- *ground sheet.*

2   **At the start of an idea** – providing what comes after the colon is a continuation of what was said before the colon or is an explanation of it. Like a list, what comes before the colon should make sense if written on its own.

The chef had everything under control: dinner would be ready soon.
Dad thought the car was cool: he'd always wanted a Porsche.

The above examples could be written without the colon but the message would not be as forceful.

Exercises

Tick the sentences which use the colon correctly.

The spell: was magical and fantastic. ☐

I love visiting Paris: the Eiffel Tower is spectacular when lit up at night. ☐

To bake a cake you need:
- flour
- butter
- sugar. ☐

I enjoy reading:
- horror
- science fiction
- comedy
- whodunnit. ☐

Go and do!

- Make a list of six of your favourite foods. Write the list using a colon. Remember, the words before the colon should make sense on their own.
- Make a list of your favourite books or television programmes. Then write a sentence about each of the items, using a colon.
- Write a sentence, with a colon, about each of the following:

• Dracula	• horses	• Spain
• football	• music	• mobile phones.

High 5!

- I can use a colon, with bullet points if necessary, when writing a list. ☐ ☐ ☐
- I can use a colon at the start of an idea. ☐ ☐ ☐

Check-up tasks

Ask your child to make a vertical list of six things he or she would take on holiday, using a colon and bullet points.

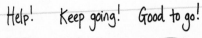
Help!   Keep going!   Good to go!

◯   ◯   ◯

Semicolons

> ## This section will:
>
> - explain when you should use a semicolon in your writing.

Top Tips for Parents

- Youngsters do find understanding and using semicolons difficult, so have patience if your child is one of them. Praise each correct usage and encourage him or her to look for places in their writing where they can be used.

- The internet gives more information on semicolons. Some sites will also give examples for the learner to work through. They tend to be more for adults but you should be able to find some suitable for younger age groups.

The power of semicolons?

Many people find using semicolons very difficult and lots of mistakes are made. Because of this people often miss them out altogether when writing rather than misuse them. When used correctly, however, semicolons can be very powerful and will impress teachers, universities and prospective employers.

Semicolons are used in the following situations:

1 **To tidy up a complicated list.**

In the house was Ada Brown, grandmother, Tom Brown, grandfather, Janet Brown, mother, Colin Brown, son and Susie Brown, daughter.

This sentence is easier to read and understand when written with semicolons.

In the house was Ada Brown, grandmother; Tom Brown, grandfather; Janet Brown, mother; Colin Brown, son and Susie Brown, daughter.

2 **To separate two closely related clauses.** A clause is a part of a sentence that contains both a subject and a verb. Each clause should be able to stand on its own. If one of the clauses does not make sense on its own then do not use a semicolon.

I enjoy listening to music; rock music relaxes me. **Correct** – the two clauses are related and each clause makes sense on its own, so this is correct use of a semicolon.

I enjoy listening to music; especially rock music. **Wrong** – although the two clauses are related, the second clause does not make sense on its own.

Our dog loves playing in the park; chasing sticks is his favourite thing to do. **Correct** – the two clauses are related and each clause makes sense on its own, so this is correct use of a semicolon.

Our dog loves chasing sticks in the park; football is a good game. **Wrong** – the two clauses are not related.

Exercises

Put a tick next to the sentences where the semicolon has been used correctly.

1 My sister is a fussy eater; she refuses to eat bananas. ☐

2 We are going to Spain this year; I love Spanish beaches. ☐

3 I would love to go to Disneyworld; my family likes walking. ☐

4 I like visiting our local museum; especially the fossil exhibition. ☐

 ## Go and do!

- Look in the kitchen cupboards, fridge or freezer.
  Note down at least six different things. Write a
  sentence that lists each of the things you've chosen,
  along with the brand. Use semicolons to separate
  each item. Look at the following example:
  *In our cupboards there is jam, Baxter's; peas, Birds
  Eye; bread, Warburton's; cornflakes, Kellogg's;
  coffee, Nescafé and tea, Lipton's.*

- Think of your favourite television programme. Write some statements about it. Join two
  of the clauses together, using semicolons, to make complete sentences. An example is
  given below. Try to make at least four complete sentences.
  The Simpsons is about a cartoon American family; Bart Simpson is my favourite character.

 ## High 5!

- I can correctly use a semicolon when writing a list.   ☐ ☐ ☐

- I can use a semicolon to separate two related clauses.   ☐ ☐ ☐

Check-up tasks

Ask your child to punctuate the following using semicolons.

Help!   Keep going!   Good to go!

- Some of my favourite soaps on television are *Eastenders*
  BBC *Coronation Street* STV *Hollyoaks* Channel 4 and
  Neighbours Channel 5.   ◯   ◯   ◯

Ask them to say which of the following is correctly punctuated.

- I love playing sport; football is great exercise.
- I love playing sport; perhaps you do too.   ◯   ◯   ◯
- I love playing sport; my friend has a dog.

Similes

This section will:

- explain what similes are.
- show how similes can be used to enhance your writing.

Top Tips for Parents

- It is easy to confuse similes with metaphors. See the section on metaphors (pages 32–33) to clarify the difference.
- www.worsleyschool. net/socialarts/simile/ page.html is an ideal site to test your child's understanding of similes.
- The internet gives good sites with long lists of similes. Try: www.saidwhat.co.uk/ spoon/similes.php

What are similes?

Similes are figures of speech. They are used to compare one thing with something else that is completely unrelated. Similes contain either the word 'like' or 'as'. They emphasise what you are trying to say about someone or something.

The room was <u>*as cold as ice*</u>.
This simile explains just how cold the room was. It would take more than a jumper to keep you warm here.

Jack ran <u>*like the wind*</u>.
Jack is obviously a very fast runner if he can go at this speed.

The girl was <u>*as pretty as a picture*</u>.
We often like pictures because of their beauty. The girl was pretty enough for this to be true.

Similes can be used to great effect in imaginative writing. Including at least one simile in each piece of imaginative writing will make your writing more interesting and descriptive.

Exercises

Choose suitable words from the box to complete the following similes below:

- As old as the ...
- As hungry as a ...
- As tall as a ...
- As daft as a ...
- Like water off a ...
- Like two peas in a ...

chimney	wolf	pod
brush	duck's back	hills

Underline the similes in the following sentences.

1   The hungry children crowded around the picnic like flies round a honey pot.

2   The angry man roared like a lion.

3 The night was cold and black as pitch.

4 Mum was as sick as a dog when she forgot to buy a lottery ticket.

 Go and do!

- Look through books and magazines to find some similes. Write down the sentence containing the simile, underline the simile then circle the phrase it's describing, e.g. *The fairy lights made the (park) look like a magical wonderland.*

- Look at the following picture. Describe these parts of the creature using similes.
  - Nose
  - Ears
  - Feet
  - Wings
  - Teeth
  - Tail

- Look through the kitchen cupboards and fridge. Make a list of as many different types of food and drink as you can. Now write a simile beside each item to describe what you feel about their taste, colour, smell, etc.
  - Peas as green as grass.
  - Curry paste as hot as fire.

- Draw a picture of a seaside scene. Use lots of detail and colour. Include children playing on the beach and in the sea, parents sunbathing, dogs running around, seagulls in the air, ice-cream sellers, etc. Now make a list of as many similes as you can to describe your picture. Remember to use your senses to describe what you see, hear and smell. Once you have your list write a paragraph about your picture, choosing one or two of your best similes.

High 5!

- I can identify similes in a piece of writing.

☐ ☐ ☐

- I can use similes to make my writing more interesting and improve description.

☐ ☐ ☐

Check-up tasks

Help!   Keep going!   Good to go!

Find some interesting pictures in magazines or old photos. Ask your child to describe what they see in them using similes.

◯ ◯ ◯

Ask your child to find the similes in the following sentences and to say what they are describing.

- Pam thought she saw a ghost. She was as white as a sheet.
- The meat was as tough as old boots.

◯ ◯ ◯

Connectives

This section will:

- explain what connectives are and how they can be used effectively in your writing.

What are connectives?

Connectives are words that join two sentences or clauses together. In the past they were called 'conjunctions' but nowadays they have the more modern name of 'connectives'. Connectives can appear at the beginning or in the middle of sentences.

It was raining. I took my umbrella.

- *Because it was raining I took my umbrella.*
- *I took my umbrella because it was raining.*
- *It was raining so I took my umbrella.*

Some connectives are simple to use. These include *and*, *but*, *so*, *because*, *if* and *then*.

Many connectives are more complex. As your writing matures in style so the connectives you use should also show your developing maturity. There will always be a place for the easier connectives, but you should demonstrate that we have the ability and understanding to use the more complex connectives as well. These include *also*, *although*, *additionally*, *finally*, *however*, *meanwhile*, *nevertheless*, *eventually*, *wherever* and *despite*.

 ## Exercises

Underline the connectives in the following sentences.

1 I always go to Madame Tussaud's whenever I visit London.

2 Despite breaking my leg, I enjoyed my skiing holiday.

3 Ben wanted a pet, however, his parents didn't like animals.

4 Sarah went to the shops while Chris went swimming.

5 Carly bought a new coat so as to stay warm in winter.

6 Before setting off, mum made us lunch.

Choose a suitable connective to join the following pairs of sentences. Don't forget you can change the order of the sentences. Can you use some more complex connectives?

1   Angus liked apples. Dad bought a big bag of them.

2   The dog barked all night in the garden. No one let him in.

3   The electricity was cut. We used candles for light.

 ## Go and do!

- Use the following website to create a list of connectives you could use in your writing. www.primaryresources.co.uk/english/englishB12.htm

- Rewrite your list in three columns. The first should include any easy connectives, the second, more difficult connectives and the third, the most complex.

- Cut some pieces of card – about the size of playing cards. Write each connective on one of the cards and place the numbers 1, 2 or 3 in the bottom corner of each card depending on the column you placed them in. Place the pile of cards upside-down in the centre of the table. If you need extra connectives, select some from the examples on page 30.

- Play a connectives game with a partner. Pick up a card and use the connective on it to make a sentence. If your partner agrees it is a good sentence, you score the value on the card – 1, 2 or 3. If you cannot make a sentence, or your partner says it is a poor sentence, then you lose the points shown on the card. Who has the higher score after six or more cards each?

 ## High 5!

- I understand what connectives are and how to use them in my writing.   ☐ ☐ ☐

- I can use a variety of connectives in my writing, including some that are more challenging.   ☐ ☐ ☐

Check-up tasks

Select some challenging connectives. Ask your child to put each one in a sentence. Can he or she use them in the middle and at the beginning of the sentences?

Help!   Keep going!   Good to go!

Metaphors

This section will:

- explain what a metaphor is
- explain the difference between a simile and a metaphor
- help you create metaphors to use in your own writing.

What are metaphors?

Metaphors, like similes, are figures of speech which compare one thing with something that is completely different. Unlike similes, however, they do not contain the words 'like' or 'as'.

We stood at the <u>foot of the mountain</u>.
We all know that mountains don't have feet but we are comparing the bottom of the mountain to the bottom of our bodies – feet.

The children were <u>buzzing with excitement</u>.
This metaphor compares the noise of excited children to the noise of bees.

Dad <u>was a dragon</u> when angry.
Dad obviously isn't a dragon but when angry he certainly seems like one.

Metaphors are stronger than similes. Similes acknowledge that what they are comparing are only similar, not actually the same. Metaphors are saying they **are** the same. Using at least one metaphor in a piece of writing can make the finished work more powerful and exciting.

 ## Exercises

Underline the metaphor in each of the following sentences.

- It was raining cats and dogs.
- The girl was the apple of her father's eye.
- After the accident the boy's face was chalk-white.
- Tom's legs had turned to rubber, preventing him from running away from the monster.
- Mum complained that the children had bottomless pits for stomachs.
- The thief hatched a plan to steal the gems.

Go and do!

- Search the internet for sites listing metaphors. Create two lists. In the first list write down all the good metaphors you can find that you understand and which you could use in a piece of writing. In the second list write all the metaphors you don't understand.

  1 Look at the second list first. Consider what each of these metaphors could mean. Ask an adult to explain them to you. Move those you now understand, and can use in your writing, into list one. Keep list one safe to help you in future tasks.

  2 Look at list one now. Draw a cartoon-style picture to illustrate the literal meaning of some of the metaphors. You can use some of the examples given on these pages as well if you like. Look at the illustrations below to give you some ideas. How funny can you make your own pictures?

- Choose a favourite book or television programme. Write three metaphors about some of the characters in it. Can you come up with some original ideas? Make sure they are metaphors and not similes! Look at the examples below.

  1 Lisa was so embarrassed by Bart's behaviour her face was a beetroot.

  2 When angry, Homer blew his top.

  3 Madge's face was a picture when she heard Lisa sing.

 ## High 5!

- I can differentiate between similes and metaphors. ☐ ☐ ☐

- I can successfully use metaphors in my writing to improve description and detail. ☐ ☐ ☐

Check-up tasks

Help!   Keep going!   Good to go!

Ask your child to explain the difference between similes and metaphors.

◯ ◯ ◯

Show your child the following sentences. Ask him or her to say which contains a simile and which contains a metaphor.

- The soldier, in camouflage gear, slithered across the ground.
- Dad roared like a lion when he dropped the stone on his foot.

◯ ◯ ◯

Alliteration

This section will:

- explain the difference between alliteration and rhyme
- demonstrate how using alliteration can enhance your writing.

Top Tips for Parents

- Encourage your child to look for alliteration in what they are reading. The more they recognise alliteration the more readily they will use it in their own writing.
- There are many internet sites which can help with alliteration. Why not try: www.nanascorner. com/2010/05/16/ alliteration-games- 6-games-to-learn- alliteration/

What is alliteration?

Alliteration is a series of two or more words in a sentence that start with the same letter.

Len laughed loudly.

Alliteration is the opposite of rhyme. Rhyme has a repetition of sound at the end of words; alliteration has a repetition of sound at the start of words.

Alliteration	Rhyme
brown bridge	*smart cart*
massive mountain	*damp camp*
dirty, dingy dress	*wet pet*
tall tree-trunk	*cool pool*

Using the occasional alliterative phrase in your writing will instantly raise its quality. However, do not overuse alliteration as this will spoil the final piece of work.

Tongue-twisters can be very good examples of alliteration.

Sister Susie sewing shirts for sailors.

Peter Piper picked a peck of pickled pepper.

She saw seashells on the seashore.

Betty Botter bought some butter, but she said, 'The butter's bitter.'

Go and do!

- Write down any other tongue-twisters you know. Ask friends and family if they know any. Type 'tongue twisters for children' into a computer search engine and you will find a great many more. Try them out on your friends. How easy are they to say?

- Write three or four sentences about a character of your choice. Include an example of alliteration.

- Write the alphabet vertically on a piece of paper. Can you write an alliterative phrase beside each letter? Look at the examples below.

  A Aunt Ada always ate apples.   **B** Big brown bears bite.
  C Colin's car catches criminals.

- Design a menu for a new restaurant. There should be three starters, three main courses and three desserts to choose from. Describe each item on the menu in an alliterative way, e.g. sweet strawberry sundae. Take a piece of A4 paper, write your menu carefully and neatly in the middle and then draw and colour a decorative border around the edge of the paper. Ask a partner whether you have made the food sound appetising and appealing.

- Make a list of some of your friends. Write at least two alliterative words to describe each one. You can be funny and original but not cruel. Here are some examples:

  Smart, small Susie

  Cool, carefree Craig

  Dangerous, daring Dave

- Type 'alliteration games' into a computer search engine. Try playing some of these games with family or friends. The Travel Game is a fun one to start with.

High 5!

- I can explain what alliteration is and identify it in a piece of writing.   ☐ ☐ ☐

- I can use alliteration to create mood and atmosphere in my writing.   ☐ ☐ ☐

Check-up tasks

Help!   Keep going!   Good to go!

Ask your child to use two alliterative words to describe each of the following.

a snake   a football   the sea   themselves

Play an alliteration game with your child. Allow him or her to choose the one he or she likes best.   ◯ ◯ ◯

Does your child understand what alliteration is? Can he or she use alliteration effectively in imaginative and personal writing?   ◯ ◯ ◯

Edit and re-draft

This section will:

- explain why editing and re-drafting are important
- tell you what to concentrate on when checking your work
- link your knowledge and understanding of the dictionary and thesaurus to effective editing.

Top Tips for Parents

- Regularly check your child's work for spelling, punctuation and paragraph errors. Don't correct any yourself but encourage him or her to find the errors. Say things like: 'There are two spelling mistakes in this paragraph', or 'Check your punctuation here'.
- For some children spelling and punctuation comes easily. Unfortunately, for others it is quite a challenge. Don't fret too much if your child falls into this category, but encourage him or her to check constantly, as above. Hopefully, it should soon improve.

How important are editing and re-drafting?

We are all able to create good pieces of imaginative writing; answer questions fully, in sentences; write instructions, letters, news articles or poems. We can create informative leaflets and advertise with posters. But no matter how good a piece of work we create, we let ourselves down if we miss out important information or write details in the wrong order. If spelling, punctuation, layout and vocabulary are careless or non-existent, our writing is flawed and our grades will not reflect what we are truly capable of. We need to check our work carefully before declaring it complete. This is called editing. Editing can be boring and time-consuming. But in the long run it is always worth it. All good authors spend many hours editing their work to ensure it is the best they can do. When you read a story or follow instructions you can be sure that what you are reading has been altered and improved several times. The author has checked that what is written makes sense, is accurately punctuated and well laid out. Finally the edited piece of work will then be rewritten. This is known as re-drafting.

When checking or editing your work you should be concentrating on the following:

- Does my writing make sense?
- Have I punctuated all the sentences accurately?
- Have I used paragraphs effectively and accurately?
- Have I used connectives to vary the lengths of my sentences?
- If I have used speech, is it accurately punctuated and does it carry the story along effectively?
- Is my spelling accurate, including any ambitious vocabulary? (Don't forget to use a dictionary and thesaurus to help you with correct spelling and when choosing exciting vocabulary!)

Exercises

Look at the following passage. All punctuation has been missed out. Notice how difficult it is to read. Replace the punctuation so that the text reads easily. *John and I wanted to watch the football on television but mum said there was a good film on the other station we didn't want to watch love is golden so we offered to watch revenge of the ugly vampires instead no way said mum that's far too scary can we watch it after dinner john asked*

Go and do!

- Get a book from your bookshelf. Any book will do. Using a computer, type three paragraphs from it but miss out all the punctuation and paragraph breaks. Now close the book, remembering the page you were at, and try to replace all the punctuation and paragraphs. Open the book at the right page again and check your work. Did you get all the punctuation in the correct place and remember where the paragraphs were?

- Select a short piece of work you have previously completed. Spend some time reading over it. Can it be improved? Edit and re-draft your work.

High 5!

I can:

- check my writing makes sense ☐ ☐ ☐

- check my punctuation for accuracy ☐ ☐ ☐

- use paragraphs effectively and accurately ☐ ☐ ☐

- use connectives to vary the lengths of my sentences ☐ ☐ ☐

- check any speech is accurately punctuated and effectively carries the story along ☐ ☐ ☐

- use a dictionary to check my spelling is accurate, including any ambitious vocabulary ☐ ☐ ☐

- use a thesaurus to help me choose exciting words. ☐ ☐ ☐

Check-up tasks

How well did your child edit the passage is the exercise?

Help! Keep going! Good to go!
○   ○   ○

Layout and presentation

This section will:

- explain the importance of well-presented work
- give you tips on how to improve the layout and presentation of your work
- describe how you can use technology to enhance presentation.

The importance of good presentation

How you present your work is an indication of how you feel about not just your work but yourself. You should develop a pride in everything you do and aim to do the best you can at all times.

How we set out our work depends on the content of the work. Have a look through this book. Each section has a title and headings. Some pages have lists and most of them have bullet points. There are diagrams on several pages and there is a variety of illustrations and pictures. Many of the activities you are asked to do on these pages require you to use illustrations, bullet points, titles, headings and, above all, neatness.

Being neat isn't difficult. If you are using a pencil, use a sharp one; when drawing lines, use a ruler; leave spaces between lines and words; make letters and words all the same size. If using an unlined piece of paper, place a lined piece of paper beneath the page you are working on to help you write in straight lines. Always remember where capital letters should be – at the beginning of sentences and proper nouns but never in the middle of words.

The type and style of handwriting you use when presenting your work depends on what you are writing for. When making notes it is acceptable for your handwriting to be untidy because you will be writing quickly, but it should be neat enough to read. A completed presentation should always be well-written and neat, with an acceptable layout which suits the purpose of the task. If your work includes diagrams, maps or pictures which need to be labelled, the words should be printed, in capital or lower-case letters. The lettering should be all the same size.

As you progress through school you will be expected to use computer packages to complete assignments. Brush up on your keyboard skills and computer presentation skills whenever possible. This includes knowing how to change font styles and sizes, insert pictures and photographs, use text boxes and drawing tools, and insert page numbers and tables.

- **Practise printing neatly**
  - Use a ruler and a pencil to draw two parallel lines, about 2cm apart, lightly on a piece of paper.
  - Carefully print your name in capitals, ensuring every letter is the same height.
  - When you are happy with it, go over the lettering in pen then rub out the parallel lines.
- **Practise making notes**
  - Ask someone to talk to you for one minute. Write down what they say as quickly as possible. Remember you need to be able to read what you write.
- **Practise writing neatly**
  - Copy out a piece of your own work or copy a paragraph from a book as neatly as possible.

 # Go and do!

- Use a digital camera or mobile phone to take several pictures throughout a typical day. Ask someone to take some photos with you in them. Print out several of the best ones and use them to illustrate a report entitled 'A typical day in my life'.
- Plan your report. Look at the photos you took and make some notes on what you want to write about. Think of some good labels for your photos. Some could be serious, some witty. They could be in complete sentences or just a word or two.
- Now write your report. Give it a title, consider headings, and place each photo you have chosen in a good position. Carefully print the labels for your photos below, above or beside them. You could consider ruling a neat box around each label to make it stand out.
- Include some illustrations if you wish and don't forget to write your name at the end.

 # High 5!

- I take pride in the presentation of my work. ☐ ☐ ☐

- I can select and apply appropriate layout and conventions, e.g. headings, subheadings, lettering, bullet points, numbers, columns and different fonts to organise ideas and illustrate meaning. ☐ ☐ ☐

- I can use technology to improve the presentation of my work. ☐ ☐ ☐

Check-up tasks

Read your child's report. Is it neatly presented and well laid out, with printed labels for photos and pictures?

Help!   Keep going!   Good to go!

◯   ◯   ◯

Openings

This section will:

- give you a variety of different ideas for opening sentences and paragraphs to help make your writing more exciting.

Top Tips for Parents

- Encourage your child to look for a selection of different openings throughout several books. Discuss the strategies the authors have used to grab the reader's attention.
- Openings refer not just to the beginning of the story, but to sentences as well.

Hook your reader

It is always well worth the time and effort to consider the best way to open your stories. A good opening will grip readers from the start and make them want to continue reading. A poor opening is likely to cause readers to put your story down without reading further. The same applies to how you open sentences or paragraphs throughout your writing. Many successful authors will not start writing new books until they have thought of a great opening sentence or paragraph which will grip their readers.

Openings should vary and there are a variety of opening strategies you can use. Some are listed below.

Begin with a noun or adjective

Angry now, Dad charged up the road.

Open with a verb

Crying uncontrollably, I looked at the empty space where my bike should have been.

Start with an adverb

Cautiously Raymond moved across the room.

Use a connective

Despite the rain, Claire chose to walk to the park instead of taking the bus. It was a decision she would always regret.

Try a simile or metaphor

Floating like a cloud, the boat drifted down the river towards the sea.

Think of a feeling

Terrified, I peeked into the room

Write two examples of your own for each of the six different ways listed above to open a story.

Other ideas

As well as using the above ideas to open your story or sentence there are other ideas you could try.

- Start with dialogue – *'Help!' I cried, as I watched the man move closer to me.*
- Say 'where' – *At the top of the hill was a rickety bench.*

- Use a short sentence – *Callum jumped!*
- Try alliteration – *Silently Sarah stretched as she studied the street ahead.*
- Start with a name – *Maisie Tinker hated school.*
- Begin with a question – *Why do mothers always want to kiss you in front of friends?*

 ## Go and do!

- Look at several books you have enjoyed reading. Make a note of the strategies the authors have used to keep your attention.
- Write each of the following on a piece of card.

  1 Use a noun or adjective
  2 Use a verb
  3 Use an adverb
  4 Use a connective
  5 Use a simile or metaphor
  6 Use a feeling

- With a partner choose a topic to write about, e.g. space, football, dogs, the circus, dinosaurs, snow, chocolate, pantomime characters, the library or museum.
- Now:
  - Shuffle the six cards.
  - Choose a card and write a sentence on your chosen topic that starts with the opening on the card.
  - Continue to write the next five sentences in the same way, choosing a different card each time.
- Now try the same activity using the other suggestions – question, name, dialogue, etc.
- Who wrote the better short story – you or your partner?

 ## High 5!

- I can use different strategies, such as nouns, verbs, adverbs, connectives and similes to open my sentences. ☐ ☐ ☐
- I realise that varying the types of openings I use in my work will make it more exciting and help keep my readers interested. ☐ ☐ ☐

Check-up tasks

 Help! Keep going! Good to go!

How easy did your child find writing the different types of openings? Play the games above as often as you like. Think of a different topic each time. Encourage your child to use his or her imagination and to vary the style of openings.   ◯ ◯ ◯

Create a character

This section will:

- explain the importance of creating effective characters in your writing
- suggest ways to help you create characters which come to life in your writing
- link characterisation with similes (pages 28–29) and metaphors (pages 32–33).

Top Tips for Parents

- Before starting this topic, discuss with your child the characterisations in his or her favourite books and television programmes. What makes these characters believable?

Characterisation

The better the characters in a book, film or television programme, the more enjoyable they are to read or watch. Good characterisation should draw you into the plot or storyline and make you feel as if you are part of the story. By the end of the story or film you should feel as if you know the characters personally.

There are two areas to consider when developing a character.

- **The character's appearance, personality and relationship with other characters**
  - What does the character look like? Consider his or her age, facial expressions, how he or she walks, talks, etc.
  - What types of clothes does he or she like to wear?
  - Is this character extrovert or introvert?
  - Does the character have a sense of humour?
  - How does the character react around others?
  - What hobbies or interests might the character have that are relevant to the story?
- **The emotions the character feels**
  - What does the character smell, see, hear in certain situations and how do these make him or her feel?
  - Is the character brave, timid, anxious, angry, etc. and what causes them to feel these ways?

When creating characters, you need to use strong verbs and adjectives to build clear pictures of them in your readers' minds. Choose suitable similes and metaphors to emphasise points you wish to make about the characters' looks, personalities or feelings.

Go and do!

- Log on to the internet and go to the following website: www.buildyourwildself.com
- Try all the different outfits, skin colours, hairstyles and body parts. When you have a good grasp of what you can create, consider how you would like to portray yourself.
- Build your normal self. Work through the first five sections building your character. Give this character a name. Try to be imaginative. When satisfied, print it out and keep to one side for later.
- Now continue changing your character to develop your wild self. Click on each of the next seven sections adding bottoms, tails, ears, etc. and finally choose a suitable background. Give this character a name. Again, be imaginative. Consider this character's personality, etc. and choose a name that suits. When happy with the result, print this out too.
- Look closely at your normal self. Make notes on the appearance, personality, typical behaviour, attitude to others, etc. Consider whether this character is introvert or extrovert and how the character feels around others. Think of powerful verbs, adjectives, similes and metaphors that would help your reader understand this character even better.
- Now use these notes to write a super paragraph describing your normal self.
- Next look closely at your wild self. As before, make notes on every aspect of this character. Remember your wild self is completely different from your normal self so the description should also be completely different.
- Write a paragraph about your wild self.

High 5!

- I can use descriptive language to make characters seem real for the reader.

  ☐ ☐ ☐

- I can express thoughts and feelings.

  ☐ ☐ ☐

Check-up tasks

Help!   Keep going!   Good to go!

Read the two paragraphs written by your child.
- Has each paragraph met the criteria listed at the beginning of this section?

  ◯ ◯ ◯

- Did your child use his or her imagination when choosing names, describing emotions, appearances, feelings, etc?

  ◯ ◯ ◯

43

Setting and atmosphere

This section will:

- show a connection between settings and atmospheres and adjectives (pages 8–9), similes (pages 28–29), metaphors (pages 32–33) and alliteration (pages 34–35)

- help you create effective settings and atmospheres in your writing using adjectives, similes, metaphors and alliteration.

Top Tips for Parents

- Encourage your child to be specific about details when telling what he or she has seen or done. Slang phrases such as 'thingummy' or mentioning a door and not where the door was, should be clarified.

Using setting and atmosphere

When we watch a film or a play on television, at the theatre or the cinema, we are given a visual picture of where the story is set, the buildings or scenery around the characters, the time of day, the weather, etc. We also get a good feeling for the atmosphere being created. It could perhaps be happy, scary, threatening or dangerous. When we read a story, however, we do not have a picture to look at so we rely on the author to 'paint a picture' with words instead.

As a writer you need to use the best adjectives, similes, metaphors and alliteration to describe accurately the setting and the atmosphere in your story. Describing how your characters react to the setting will help set the atmosphere and make us feel as if we are there as well. A good writer will describe a scene using feelings and wonderful description. Then, if something scary or horrible or sad happens in the story, we will also feel scared or revolted or sad, even though we are not actually in the story. We have been transported into the story by the great description.

Remember

Remember, to create a super setting and awesome atmosphere you need to use:

- Adjectives – *The cool water lapped around his aching feet.*
- Similes – *The boggy ground was like a wet sponge.*
- Metaphors – *The rain fell in sheets, soaking them immediately.*
- Alliteration – *Marvellous, majestic mountains towered above the buildings.*

Exercises

Look at the scene below. Write five or six sentences describing the setting and atmosphere. Say what the character feels, what can be smelled or touched, etc. Don't forget to use the best adjectives, similes, metaphors and alliteration.

Go and do!

- Stand up, take your paper and a pencil and go and look out of a window.
  - Look carefully at what you see.
  - On your paper make accurate notes on everything you can see, hear, feel and smell. Note down what the weather is like, what the people, if any, are doing. Are there any animals, dogs, cats, sheep, etc? What buildings are there? If you were out in the street what might you smell – hotdogs, wet grass, rubbish? Can you hear music blaring, wind blowing, leaves rustling, traffic roaring, cows mooing, dogs yapping, people shouting?
- Now imagine you have been asked to describe the scene to someone over the phone. They are going to draw what you describe to them so you need to be as accurate as possible.
- Write a description of the scene from your window. In at least five or six of your sentences you should use excellent adjectives, similes, metaphors or alliteration.
- Ask a partner to draw what you have described. Is it similar to the scene from your window? Improve your description if necessary.

High 5!

- I can use what I've learned from other sections to create super settings and atmospheres, using adjectives, similes, metaphors and alliteration.

☐ ☐ ☐

Check-up tasks

Help!   Keep going!   Good to go!

Ask your child to find a picture in a book or magazine. Without the picture, let your child describe it to you. Can you draw the scene fairly accurately just from listening to the description of it? Encourage your child to be specific, using adjectives to help, e.g. 'a small, rickety hut on the left' is better than 'a small hut'.

◯   ◯   ◯

Create a cliffhanger

This section will:

- explain what cliffhangers are and why they are used in writing
- encourage you to look for cliffhangers in written stories, TV dramas, etc.
- encourage you to use cliffhangers in your own writing to add suspense.

Action rules

Many years ago, when the film industry was in its infancy, people flocked to cinemas to see films. There were no televisions, videos or DVDs in those days so films were extremely popular. These films were in black and white and had no sound, just action, hence the popular name 'movies'. As there was no sound, the story was told through action. Stories were told, and feelings portrayed, by exaggerated facial expressions and over-the-top performances. Saturday mornings at the cinema were the time when children went to see films; they were the highlights of their week. To make sure they kept coming back Saturday after Saturday, film-makers created storylines that would continue for several weeks; a bit like the television soaps of today. Each week the story would end with the hero or heroine in a dangerous predicament. If people wanted to find out what happened next, they had to return to the cinema the following week. These predicaments included such things as the heroine being tied to a train track with a train approaching at top speed, and the hero being pushed out of the window of a high-rise building or dangling off the side of a steep cliff. After a while these types of endings became known as 'cliffhangers', regardless of whether anyone was actually hanging from a cliff.

Cliffhangers are used today by many writers. They create suspense and hold the reader's attention, encouraging us to continue reading to find out what happens next.

The following example of a cliffhanger appears at the end of a chapter in a magical adventure story. To find out what happens next the reader would need to read the next chapter.

He stopped talking as Arthur stopped walking. Both had heard the same thing. A stealthy step behind them, the soft zing of clockwork and the faint switch of air, as if it had been disturbed by something moving up and down.

Something like an axe ...

Garth Nix, *Mister Monday*

As well as setting the scene with a great description, using a superb choice of vocabulary, the author has used punctuation – an ellipsis – to create his cliffhanger. An ellipsis is the three dots at the end of an uncompleted sentence. An ellipsis lets the reader know that something is about to happen, but to find out what this is you need to read on.

 ## Exercises

Not all the chapters of a story end with cliffhangers. Read the following possible chapter endings. Mark the ones you think are good cliffhangers.

1 The water was rising steadily. All the rain of the past week had swollen the river, which was close to bursting its banks. She knew she had to reach the shore quickly. It was dark now and, recalling the rumours of locals disappearing in mysterious circumstances, she did not want to stay in the water a moment longer than was necessary. Suddenly she felt something grab her ankle with a vice-like grip. Rosie screamed …

2 Eddie walked up the path. The sun was shining, birds were singing and his family were safe and well. He just knew this was going to be a great day.

3 Donny had the ball at his feet. There was no one between him and the goal. Victory was his, he thought. Unfortunately, he had not counted on what happened next!

 ## Go and do!

- Write three different possible cliffhanger endings. Remember, do not copy what you find in other books, but use the way the authors create and develop cliffhangers in their writing to write cliffhangers of your own.

 ## High 5!

- I understand what a cliffhanger is and why writers use them.

- I can use a cliffhanger in my writing to create suspense.

Check-up tasks

Help! Keep going! Good to go!

Is your child able to recognise cliffhangers in stories?

Read the cliffhangers your child has written. Has he or she understood what they needed to do?

Autobiography

This section will:

- explain the difference between biographies and autobiographies
- help you plan and write your own autobiography.

Top Tips for Parents

- Before starting this task, look for some autobiographies in a library or bookshop that would be suitable for your child to read, e.g. Roald Dahl's *Boy*.
- Talk about your child's life so far. Tell stories about his or her early childhood – why you chose their name, any funny things he or she said, holidays you all enjoyed as a family, stories about family pets, etc. Encourage your child to incorporate these into an autobiography.

Life stories

Some people feel that they have had such interesting lives or done such interesting things that they should write their life stories down for the rest of us to read and enjoy. Sometimes they get other authors to write their story for them. These stories are called **biographies**. If they write their own stories, however, these are called **autobiographies**.

An autobiography tells us many things about the person who wrote it. We learn about his or her early years, his or her family and what life was like for him or her at school. We read about his or her likes and dislikes, feelings, hobbies and, of course, what he or she is famous for.

Read the following extract taken from an autobiography of a famous poet.

I went to two primary schools and two secondary schools. The second primary school, which I went to between the ages of seven and eleven, had just been built – a brand new school, with a big playground. I was in a class of about 48 children. We all sat in rows of desks, four rows of 12.

I was no good at all at maths, but I loved writing stories and anything to do with animals. I once took photos of the ducks in the park and wrote a little piece about each photo, and the teacher put it up on the wall. I was very proud of that.

Michael Rosen, *All About Me*

Go and do!

Think about your own life, your family, pets and friends. What have you done that was sad or exciting? What are your likes and dislikes, hobbies and interests? Make notes about your life under the following headings:

- early years
- family and friends
- school years
- hobbies and interests
- hopes for the future
- anything else of interest such as holidays, parties, illnesses etc. These should be listed at your planning stage, showing your age at the time, e.g. *age seven – went to Disney World, birthday party at McDonald's, caught measles.* (Don't worry if you or your family cannot remember your exact age: a good guess will do.)

Now write your autobiography, using your notes to help you. Start a new chapter for each of your headings. Include feelings where necessary. Write your life story on the computer if possible. If you have access to photographs, insert them in the relevant places or use suitable clip art. This will enhance as well as illustrate your autobiography. If you are unable to insert photographs using the computer, leave spaces where you can attach actual photos or drawings once you have printed your work.

Edit your work carefully before printing it out. Create an attractive front cover. Give your autobiography a special title and don't forget to add your name as the author. If you wish, you could add a back cover with 'blurb'.

High 5!

- I understand, and can explain, the difference between a biography and an autobiography.

☐ ☐ ☐

- I can write my autobiography detailing many interesting facts in the correct order.

☐ ☐ ☐

- I can include a title, dates and headings.

☐ ☐ ☐

- I can illustrate my work using photographs, pictures or drawings.

☐ ☐ ☐

Check-up tasks

Help!   Keep going!   Good to go!

Read your child's autobiography. How accurate and detailed is it? Remember it is how he or she sees his or her life, which may not be quite how you see it.

◯   ◯   ◯

Posters

This section will:

- give the purpose of posters
- explain how to create an effective poster.

Poster power

Posters are used to advertise, persuade or simply to decorate. They give useful information about forthcoming events, missing animals or people, shops, venues, new products, etc. Posters that advertise are asking us to do something, such as buy a ticket for an event, turn on the TV and watch, go and see something, and so on.

Any posters should:

- be eye-catching
- be clearly laid out
- include all necessary information and be well-organised but not cluttered
- use words and phrases specific to the topic and genre
- include pictures if necessary.

 ## Exercises

Look at the two posters here. Talk to a partner about why one is a good poster and the other is not.

 ## Go and do!

1   Look through old comics and magazines. Cut out any adverts you think are good. (Ask first if the material is not your own.) You should choose them because they are examples of good adverts, not because you like the products they are advertising. Talk to someone about why you chose these examples. Keep them to refer to in future tasks.

2 Using a piece of card or heavy paper – A4 size is ideal – create an advert for a new sweet. On a piece of scrap paper draw a picture of the sweet. Write down any ideas you have for a good name for the product, what it tastes like and why people should buy it. Can you include some alliteration when describing it? For example, 'terrific-tasting toffee' or 'fruity-flavoured fudge'. Underline or highlight all the ideas you want to use in your poster. Now create your poster, remembering to follow the criteria on page 50.

3 Create an advert for something you wish to sell. This advert will be displayed in the local paper or newsagent's window. Think of something you no longer use because it is broken, or you have outgrown it. (Why not be creative and sell your big brother or little sister?) On a piece of planning paper, write down what you are selling and make two lists. The first list should mention everything that is positive about the item. Consider colour, size, suitable age, condition, etc. The second list should include all the negative points about the object, e.g. broken or missing pieces, pages torn or missing, noisy. If possible, write your advert onto a blank white postcard. However, if this is not available draw a postcard-sized box on a sheet of paper and write your advert inside the box. Word your advert carefully so as not to put people off buying the thing you are trying to sell. Perhaps you could turn some of the negative points into good selling points, e.g. a dog that barks a lot might be advertised as 'Keeps unwanted guests away'. Don't forget to mention how potential buyers can contact you.

High 5!

I can create posters that:

- are eye-catching ☐ ☐ ☐

- are clearly laid out ☐ ☐ ☐

- include all the necessary information and are well organised but not cluttered ☐ ☐ ☐

- use words and phrases specific to topic and genre ☐ ☐ ☐

- include pictures if necessary. ☐ ☐ ☐

Check–up tasks

Help!　Keep going!　Good to go!

Ask your child to create a poster advertising a vacancy for a spy. (You can, if you prefer, choose something you know your child is interested in.) You should outline the following criteria for your child but allow him or her to work on their own. The finished poster should include:

- a heading
- a picture
- relevant attributes for potential applicants
- where to apply for this job

○　　○　　○

Leaflets

> ## This section will:
>
> * explain the purpose of leaflets
> * give the criteria essential for good leaflets
> * show the link between leaflets and the section called 'Persuade or argue?' (pages 92–93).

What are leaflets used for?

Leaflets are designed to advertise and give information about clubs, shops, attractions, etc. Prospective MPs and local councillors advertise themselves as suitable candidates for election by posting leaflets through doors, explaining why they are the best people for the job. Take-away food outlets advertise by including leaflets in local papers. Leaflets are used to encourage you to buy, visit, join or vote for whatever is being advertised in them. They are powerful, persuasive tools.

Leaflets should:

* give clear, concise information
* be well laid out
* have titles and subheadings
* include only relevant points, in order, with nothing important missed out
* be illustrated with pictures, diagrams or photos where necessary
* include contact details such as addresses, phone numbers and email addresses.

Gather a selection of leaflets from papers, magazines, mail shots, etc. Separate them into piles depending on what is being advertised. Read through each pile. Make a note on the similarities and differences between the piles.

 ## Go and do!

* Consider a hobby or interest you have. Take a piece of A4 paper and fold it either in half or into three. Create a leaflet for other people your age, explaining where they can go to enjoy this hobby, what equipment is needed, any special clothing that is required, the cost, etc. If this is a club, e.g. swimming, you will need to mention such things as the days when the club is on, times for different levels and groups, appropriate ages, etc. Ask a friend to comment on your leaflet. Have you included all the relevant information?

- Imagine that friends of yours are opening a restaurant and that they have asked you to design a leaflet advertising this new venture.

  Consider:
  - What is different about this restaurant? Perhaps the menu features only seafood or crocodile meat? Maybe the décor is all green? Maybe it has a jungle theme?
  - What type of food will they be serving?
  - Is the restaurant a take-away? Do customers eat in? Or both?
  - Are they trying to encourage a certain market, e.g. vegetarian, teenage or older adult?

  Create a leaflet, using a computer if you wish, advertising this unique venture. Remember that you want to encourage people to visit the restaurant, so make the leaflet as attractive as possible. Don't forget to include the name of the restaurant, titles, the address, phone numbers for booking purposes and of course plenty of mouth-watering pictures of the food the restaurant serves!

- Consider where you live. Make a list of places in your area children your age would enjoy visiting. Create a leaflet advertising one of these venues. Mention where this place of interest is, why it is interesting, who would enjoy it, etc. The title, headings and pictures are important.

✋ High 5!

- I understand what leaflets are designed to do.

- I can create leaflets that:
  - give clear, concise information   ☐ ☐ ☐

  - are well laid out with titles and sub-headings   ☐ ☐ ☐

  - have all the relevant points in the correct order, with bullet points, pictures and diagrams as necessary.   ☐ ☐ ☐

Check-up tasks

Help!   Keep going!   Good to go!

Discuss the following points with your child:
- the variety of things leaflets are used for
- the criteria for writing a successful leaflet.

◯ ◯ ◯

Look at the leaflets your child wrote for the above tasks. Read over them and ask your child how they think they have done against the set criteria. Would he or she alter or improve anything if asked to write them again? Give your assessment of the leaflets. Be positive but offer some constructive advice where necessary.

◯ ◯ ◯

Reading for information

This section will:

- explain ways to help you find information quickly and efficiently by using an index correctly, and skimming and scanning
- link the skills of reading for information to researching and reporting (pages 68–69).

(pages 68–69)

Top Tips for Parents

- Reading for information is an essential skill. Help your child develop this skill by encouraging him or her to use the contents pages and indices of reference books. Try not to point out these pages. Check that he or she remembers that if a word begins with, for example, 'w' not to start at the beginning of the index.

Why read?

We read for two main reasons.

1 Enjoyment

Reading gives many people a great deal of pleasure.

There is nothing better than being able to relax and lose yourself in a good book.

2 Information

Reading is necessary for learning. We use our reading skills countless times each day without always realising it. For example, we read bus and train timetables, television listings in the paper, road signs and directions, maps, recipes, instructions, street names, shop names and product names. We rely on our reading skills to help us through every day.

When using reference books, referring to the indices or contents pages will help you find the chapters or pages you need. Remember that indices will be in alphabetical order, so don't waste time looking through letters that are not relevant to the words you are looking for. Go immediately to the sections where you will find the word or words you're looking for.

Skim reading – skim reading involves quickly reading, noting only the important points.

Scanning the page – scanning involves quickly reading an article to find the section you need. You will then take more care and time to read this part. Information not required for the given task is ignored, allowing you to concentrate only on what is important at the time.

When reading for information, the better your reading skills are, the quicker and more efficient the task will be. Skilled readers do not read every word. They skim and scan pages and articles to find the information they require. They will then read these parts carefully. The more you read, the easier it is to skim and scan and the less time you waste reading irrelevant material. Reading for information is not simply about copying pages from books or the internet, but extracting the necessary information and ignoring the unnecessary detail.

Exercises

- Read the following extract (skim read if possible) then complete the given task.

*The life cycle of the butterfly is even more complicated, with four stages. It starts life as an egg that hatches into a caterpillar. The caterpillar feeds all the time, so it grows quickly. Finally, the caterpillar becomes a **pupa**. The pupa does not move and has a tough protective covering. It looks as if nothing is happening, but inside, the body of the caterpillar is changing into one of an adult butterfly. The body shape changes and the wings grow. Then the pupal case splits and an adult butterfly emerges.*

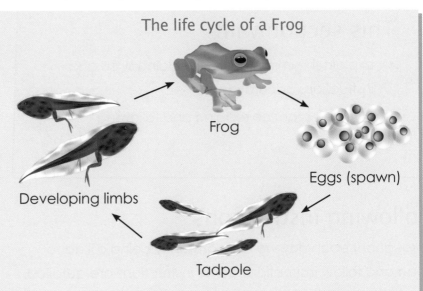

The life cycle of a Frog

Frog

Eggs (spawn)

Developing limbs

Tadpole

Sally Morgan, *Life Cycles*

Using the information in the passage, draw and label a picture of the life cycle of a butterfly. Give the diagram a title.

Go and do!

Use the internet or reference books to find the answers to the following questions:
- What is the longest river in the world?
- What is the world's largest gorge?
- Which is the world's longest mountain range?
- Where is the driest place on Earth?
- Where is the longest wall in the world?
- Which is the world's deepest lake?

High 5!

- I can skim and scan text to find key words and specific information. ☐ ☐ ☐

Check-up tasks

Help! Keep going! Good to go!

Hand your child a reference book. Ask him or her to use the index to find certain pieces of information. Can he or she find the pages quickly, using their knowledge of the alphabet? If you ask him or her to find a person, do they look for the surname, not the first name?

Reading and following instructions

This section will:

- explain the importance of reading signs and instructions accurately
- give you practice reading and following instructions.

Following instructions

Throughout each day we are constantly being asked to read and follow instructions. Some instructions are detailed, involving a lot of reading. Others are very short, often just a few words, or perhaps a picture. There are road signs telling us such things as where to cross the road, which roads are one-way traffic only, and which streets are for pedestrians only. In shopping malls there are signs showing us where to park, and where to find changing rooms or the toilets. Signs are important, so we need to know how to read them and follow the instructions they are giving us.

 Exercises

Think of your school. Make a list of the signs you see:

- around the outside
- in your classroom
- around the corridors, gym hall, dining room, etc.

Do any of these signs have illustrations or symbols? Draw some of them.

Instructions are important for other things as well. Often we buy furniture or games that require us to build them. Instructions are important as they tell us the order in which we should fix parts together, as well as which part goes where. Instructions should be read very carefully.

If we do not have the instructions then assembling things can be very difficult or even impossible! Imagine being given a new bicycle with the assembly instructions missing. How frustrating would it be? All you want to do is go out with your friends and enjoy yourself but instead you're wondering if a particular piece should be attached to the pedal or to the saddle!

Go and do!

- Ask a friend or family member to draw a detailed picture or ask them to find a suitable picture in a magazine, book or on the internet. You can do the same.
- Listen to your friend describe the picture they have drawn or chosen and try to draw the picture he or she describes. How well has it been described to you? Do the two pictures look similar?
- Ask him or her to redraw your picture. Describe your picture carefully, remembering to use positional instructions such as:

  - in the bottom right-hand corner
  - sitting on the top branch of the tree
  - beside the house
  - under the chair
  - towards the back of the room.

Have you described your picture with enough accuracy for your friend to create an almost identical one?

 ## High 5!

- I can share information and explain processes when listening and talking. □ □ □

- I can read and follow instructions, carrying them out in the correct order if necessary, missing nothing important out. □ □ □

Check-up tasks

Help!   Keep going!   Good to go!

Give your child a piece of A4 paper and show him/her the following instructions. Say there is one minute to complete the task. Time your child but offer no help or assistance.

1 Read all the instructions.
2 Write your name at the top of the page in the middle.
3 Underline your name.
4 Write your age in the bottom right-hand corner.
5 Draw a square in the middle of the page.
6 Inside the square write the name of a friend.
7 Under the square write the number of the house you live in.
8 Draw a straight line across the centre of the page.
9 If you are a boy write a capital H in the bottom left corner. If you are a girl write a capital M in the bottom left corner.
10 Do only instructions 1, 2 and 3.

Writing instructions

This section will:

- explain the correct procedure for writing instructions.

Writing instructions

As well as being able to read instructions, it is also important that we learn how to write instructions. Instructions that are confusing, with important information missed out or in the wrong order, can render what we are trying to do useless. When writing instructions we should remember the following:

- Always describe in detail the materials and equipment needed.

  It is no use trying to bake a cake if we do not have all the necessary ingredients to hand or the bowls, mixers, etc. to make it.

- Instructions need to be clear, in the correct order and well-organised.

- Number each step or use bullet points to help readers easily follow them. Make sure the instructions are in the correct order with nothing important missed out, e.g. if paper needs to be cut or folded make sure you say where and how big a cut or fold.

- Start your instructions with a suitable title. Headings such as 'What you need' and 'What you do', as well as pictures and diagrams, will all help the reader follow your instructions.

- Begin each step of your instructions with a 'command' verb, e.g. *Get*, *Slice*, *Take*. Suitable adverbs can be placed before the verb, e.g. **Carefully** slice.

- Diagrams and illustrations can be included with the instructions where necessary to give readers a better understanding of what to do or what the finished item should look like.

Go and do!

- Look in kitchen cupboards, on supermarket shelves, at adverts in magazines, and make a list of ingredients you could use to write instructions for a magic potion, an ogre's sandwich, a pet's dinner or your own choice of strange meal. You can be as imaginative and funny as you like.

1 Remembering to follow the criteria set out above, write instructions for the recipe you have chosen to create on a piece of rough paper.

2 Read your recipe carefully. Could it be improved? Have you included instructions for mixing or stirring? Did you use adverbs such as 'stir **slowly**', 'mix **vigorously**' or 'slice **thinly**'?

3 Now check the headings. You should have a title explaining what the recipe is for and headings such as 'What you need' and 'What to do'.

4 Finally, when you are completely happy with the recipe, re-write it neatly on paper or card. Draw and colour a decorative border around the edge and include a picture of how the finished potion or meal should look, along with any other instructions, such as 'Store under the bed until covered in mould' or 'Use before the weekend'.

5 Show your recipe to family or friends. Are they suitably impressed? Could they follow the instructions easily?

High 5!

When writing instructions I remember to:

- include titles and suitable headings ☐ ☐ ☐

- write them in detail in the correct order ☐ ☐ ☐

- ensure nothing important is missed out ☐ ☐ ☐

- include diagrams and illustrations. ☐ ☐ ☐

Check-up tasks

Help!   Keep going!   Good to go!

Select or copy a recipe for a pizza or a favourite family dish. The steps for making the dish should be simple to follow and easy to understand. Cut the steps up and present the mixed-up pieces to your child. Ask him or her to place the recipe back in the correct order and stick it onto paper or card. How easy did your child find this task?

◯   ◯   ◯

Create a game

This section will:

- explain the importance of rules and instructions in a game
- list points to consider when writing rules.

Think about games

Many people love playing board games. There are games for all ages and all interests. We can buy games for people who love using words, games for people who enjoy drawing and games for those who like solving mysteries. Some games challenge us, making us think before giving an answer or making a move. Others simply give us a great deal of fun and laughter. There are games the whole family can play and games suitable for adults or children only. Choosing a good game can be difficult. Adverts try to convince us that this is the game we must have. The packaging tells that the game is fantastic, but very often we discover that games are either too complicated, too easy or just plain boring.

Think of the games you enjoy playing. One of the most important aspects of any game is the rules. Without them we would find playing the game almost impossible. There are several points we need to know when setting up a game for the first time.

- What age is the game suitable for?
- How many people can play the game?
- What do you need to play the game – dice, counters, spinner, timer or anything else?
- How is the first player chosen?
- How is the game played?
- Are there forfeits or bonuses and when do these come into play?
- How is the winner determined?

Exercises

Look at this game board. The rules and instructions have been mislaid. Create some rules for use with this board. Use the checklist above to ensure you miss nothing out. When you have finished, give the game a name. Ask someone to check your rules. Would he or she be able to play the game or have you missed anything out?

Go and do!

Create your own board game. Think of a theme you are interested in. The following list might give you some ideas but you could choose one of your own.

- Sport
- Space
- World of fashion
- Technology
- Transport
- Animals

Consider the type of layout you would like for the game, e.g. squares around the outside of the board, squares all over the board or a random path across the board.

Will your game have bonuses and forfeits? If so you will need to consider when these will be used and what will be on them, e.g. *Fall off catwalk – miss a turn* or *Have a ride in space buggy – move forward three spaces*.

Will you require dice, spinners, counters, etc for the game? Don't forget to include them and to mention them in the rules and instructions.

How many players can play the game? How is your game to be played? Do players work their way around the board or can they jump from one side to another?

What decides who the winner will be?

Plan your game on scrap paper. Sketch out the layout of the board and make notes on the rules and instructions needed for the game. Ask someone to play the game with you. Make notes on any improvements you think it needs.

Now design the final gameboard on a good piece of paper or card. Write the rules and instructions neatly and clearly. You should include the name of the game both on the board and above the instructions.

Enjoy your game.

High 5!

- I understand why rules and instructions for a game should be detailed and precise.

  ☐ ☐ ☐

- I am able to create an interesting game with detailed instructions to help make playing the game a fun experience.

  ☐ ☐ ☐

Check-up tasks

Play the game with your child. Don't ask him or her to explain the rules. Follow the rules yourself and assess how clear and easy they are. Do they satisfy the criteria set out above?

Help!   Keep going!   Good to go!

○   ○   ○

Personal letter writing

This section will:

- give the criteria necessary for writing a successful personal letter.

Top Tips for Parents

- Encourage your child to write thank-you letters for Christmas and birthday gifts. Stress how important it is to observe the basic rules of letter writing and check that he or she has missed nothing important out.

Letter rules

It is important to know how to write a good letter. There are rules for writing letters that we need to learn and use.

There are two basic types of letters – personal letters and functional letters. For the following tasks we will be looking at personal letters. Help on how to write functional letters can be found on pages 94–95.

Personal letters

We write personal letters to family and friends – letters of thanks for gifts or for favours, letters of news and interest when on holiday or when living further away.

A successful personal letter will:

- include the conventions of letter writing, for instance address, greeting and sign-off
- be written in a style that is appropriate to the intended reader.

A completed letter should have:

- the address written at the top right of the page
- the date written below the address
- your greeting written below the date but on the left-hand side
- indented paragraphs
- an informal ending, using the words 'love from', 'best wishes' or something similar
- your name at the end.

Look at this example of an informal letter.

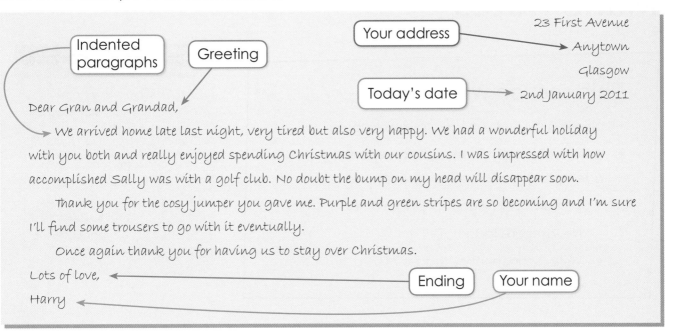

Your address → 23 First Avenue → Anytown, Glasgow

Today's date → 2nd January 2011

Indented paragraphs | **Greeting**

Dear Gran and Grandad,

We arrived home late last night, very tired but also very happy. We had a wonderful holiday with you both and really enjoyed spending Christmas with our cousins. I was impressed with how accomplished Sally was with a golf club. No doubt the bump on my head will disappear soon.

Thank you for the cosy jumper you gave me. Purple and green stripes are so becoming and I'm sure I'll find some trousers to go with it eventually.

Once again thank you for having us to stay over Christmas.

Lots of love,

Harry

Ending | **Your name**

Go and do!

- Log on to the following website:

  www.readwritethink.org/files/resources/interactives/letter_generator/

  Click on 'Friendly Letter' and follow the instructions given to complete a letter to a relative or friend. Print out the finished letter.

- Look at the pictures below. Choose two that might be given to you as birthday presents. One present should be something you would really like to receive. The other should be something you would hate to be given. If you don't fancy any of the gifts, create one of your own. Write two thank-you letters. Try to make the unwanted gift sound great but inject some humour into the letter. See the example above for ideas.

High 5!

When writing a personal letter I remember to:

- include my address, a greeting and to sign off informally

- write in paragraphs

- write my name at the end.

Check-up tasks

Read the finished letters. Check the criteria set out at the top of the first page. Has your child achieved them?

Help!   Keep going.   Good to go!

Make notes

This section will:

- give helpful hints on how to make notes
- be a useful preliminary activity before attempting the following sections:
    - Research and reporting (pages 68–69)
    - News reports (pages 70–71)
    - Write a commentary (pages 74–75).

Top Tips for Parents

- Encourage your child to use 'text speak' when making notes.
- Only important facts should be noted down. Unnecessary words need not be included. They can be added later, when writing the report, etc.

Notes are useful

Knowing how to make notes is very useful. Newspaper reporters and the police make notes when interviewing people. You will find making notes a handy tool when researching or planning a report or any other piece of writing. Note-making is an important skill to learn. There are several ways to do this.

- Think of how you text using a mobile phone. You shorten words, use letters in place of words and miss out unnecessary letters and words. The final message is clear – just not written in standard English.
- Write your notes under relevant headings. This means when you come to write your report (or whatever your task is) all the information relating to a particular point is together.
- Highlight important and relevant points. Of course, this is useful only if you have a copy of the text. Do not deface a book to do this.

Making notes takes less time and uses less space than writing everything out. It enables us to jot down quickly what we wish to remember or pass on, but we should remember to write the finished report or other piece of writing in standard English.

No matter which method of note-making you use, you should always write your finished piece in your own words. Failure to do this is an offence. Passing another author or writer's work off as your own is called **plagiarism**. As you make notes, jot down the books and websites you used and the authors' names. If you include a quote from another source in your own work you must say where it has come from and who wrote it.

Exercises

Imagine you are a police officer. Look at this crime scene. Make notes on everything you see. Remember, as a police officer you may be asked to report back to a superior or judge, so look carefully and miss nothing out in your notes. Talk to a partner about your notes. Did you notice all the relevant details? Close this book and write out the report you would hand to your boss. Do not look at the picture until you have completed it. Use only the notes you made. If you made good notes this task should be very easy!

Go and do!

With a partner, watch the news on television. As you watch, listen carefully and make notes on one of the main items. Using your notes, write out a report on the item in standard English. Your partner should check to make sure that your report includes all the relevant points from the item, and that they are in the correct order. How well did you do? Check your partner's notes. Did you make a note of something he or she didn't? How good are your listening skills?

High 5!

- I can make good notes and use them to help me create my own text.

- I can organise my notes appropriately.

- I understand I must acknowledge my sources of information.

□ □ □

□ □ □

□ □ □

Check-up tasks

Help! Keep going! Good to go!

Talk to your child about something you have done recently. Ask him or her to make notes as you talk and then to read the notes back to you. Did your child manage to make a note of all the important facts and to repeat them back to you in the correct order?

○ ○ ○

Questions

Why ask questions?

Being able to ask and write good, thoughtful questions is an acquired skill. Good questions require their recipients to think carefully and answer fully. Questions which require yes or no answers are fine for basic information such as, 'Are you walking home from school today?' However, when seeking detailed information we need to consider more powerful questioning techniques and formulate more enquiring questions. These fall into three categories:

- **literal.** The answers to these questions can be found in the text.

- **inferential.** The answers to these questions need to be carefully thought out. You will not find them directly in the text. You will need to look for hints and clues in the text.

- **evaluative.** These questions ask you to explain the meaning of or give an opinion on something that happened in the text.

We ask detailed questions for six main reasons.

1 To check what someone has remembered
These types of questions may begin:
- Can you find a word for …?
- How would you explain/describe/ show …?

2 To check if a person has understood
These questions may begin:
- Can you explain what is happening? (And why?)
- What do you think will happen when/if …?

3 To see if someone can apply the knowledge they have learned
These questions may begin:
- How would you show your understanding of …?
- What would happen if …?

4 To encourage someone to analyse or look closely at something
These questions may begin:
- How could you show the differences and/ or similarities?
- What evidence can you show to …?

5 To evaluate or assess someone's understanding

These questions may begin:

- Would it be better if …?
- Why did the character choose …?

6 To help someone create ideas and use his or her own imagination

These questions may begin:

- Could you invent or design a new way to …?
- How would you improve …?

 ## Go and do!

- Choose a book appropriate to your age and ability. Read it carefully. Write six questions concerning its content. Your questions need to be considered and thought-provoking. Look at the question samples above to help you formulate challenging questions of your own.

- When you are happy with the questions you have written, ask a family member or friend who has also read the book to answer them. Imagine you are an interviewer on the radio. You will need a recording device such as a computer with recording software. Introduce your 'guest' and ask your questions. Record the 'interview'. Listen to the recording. Could you improve the questions you asked? Were they challenging enough? If necessary, write some more questions or alter the original questions. Repeat the recording procedure.

 ## High 5!

- I can ask and respond to different types of question – literal, inferential and evaluative.
☐ ☐ ☐

- I have asked and answered questions to show I have an opinion on something I have listened to.
☐ ☐ ☐

- I can use my questioning skills to gather information and help my understanding.
☐ ☐ ☐

- I can create different types of questions for others to answer.
☐ ☐ ☐

Check-up tasks

Help!　Keep going!　Good to go!

Assess the quality of your child's questions. Was your child able to write questions in the styles given in this section?
◯ ◯ ◯

Ask your child some questions about something that interests him or her. Ensure that your questions encourage your child to think carefully before answering.
◯ ◯ ◯

Research and reporting

This section will:

- explain the link between research and reporting and note-making (pages 64–65) and stories/giving a talk (pages 88–89)

- explain the importance of recognising your sources of information

- give you help and advice when researching and writing your own report.

Top Tips for Parents

- All children should be encouraged to improve their report-writing skills. They will be asked to write reports for almost every subject they study. If they wish to enter further education it will be a required skill. In many professions report-writing is part of the job.

Research skills

One skill you will find of use as you go through life is the ability to research. You may need to research a topic for a school project. Often you will be asked to write a report on your research.

Depending on what the report is about, your research may take the form of:

- visiting the library and borrowing relevant books
- watching TV programmes or DVDs
- searching the internet
- talking to someone with knowledge of the subject you have to report on.

A good report will often use more than one research method.

When researching, you should make thorough notes. The best way to do this is to create a list of headings and write your notes below the relevant ones.

Finally, make a note of all your research sources. Good reports always mention where the information came from. One way of doing this is to place a small letter or number beside each piece of information, to link it to the title of the book or other source of information from which it was taken. Such a list of sources is called a bibliography. Each item in the bibliography has a number or letter beside it that links back to the information in your report.

Remember how to make notes (pages 64–65) and ask questions (pages 66–67). Re-read the relevant pages in this book if you need to refresh your memory.

Once you have researched the topic, you can write the report. The following criteria should be observed:

- The main ideas should be presented as clearly and accurately as possible.
- All information should be organised under relevant headings and clearly presented.
- The report should open with an introduction (one or two sentences explaining what the report is about) and finish with a rounding-off statement (one or two sentences that summarise the topic you are reporting on).
- Remember to include a title, headings, diagrams, numbering, etc, as appropriate to the topic.

It is essential to write the report in your own words. Downloading information from the internet or copying chunks from a book is fine for research but simply copying this information into your own report is called plagiarism. **Plagiarism is an offence**. You cannot pass another person's work off as your own. Always use your own words to write a report. If you include a quote from another source, recognise this by saying so.

 # Go and do!

- Research and write a report on space travel using the help below or check out a variety of suggestions for reports in other sections of this book, e.g. *Persuade or argue?* on pages 92–93. Choose a topic that interests you.
  - Start by logging onto the NASA kids' club:
    www.nasa.gov/audience/forkids/kidsclub/flash/index.html

Explore the site. Think of possible headings you could make notes under. Try some of the games if you need some time to unwind before settling to work.

  - For more information try: www.nasa.gov/

Write a detailed report, remembering to follow the criteria for report writing.

 # High 5!

- When researching I am able to use more than one source of information. ☐ ☐ ☐
- I have researched a topic, selected and organised information from my notes under suitable headings in a logical and structured manner, using my own and technical vocabulary. ☐ ☐ ☐
- I recognise I must acknowledge my sources of information and I am able to do this. ☐ ☐ ☐

Check-up tasks

Look at the reports your child has written. Has he or she met the criteria set out above? Has he or she written a detailed report on space travel?

Help! Keep going! Good to go!

◯   ◯   ◯

News reports

> ## This section will:
>
> - explain the purpose of news articles
> - give the criteria for successful news articles
> - link news reports with the section on making notes.

Reporting style

Writing reports for newspapers requires a different style of writing from writing ordinary reports. The newspaper reporter should merely report the facts when writing. Personal feelings should not be evident. The report should be written in the third person, i.e. it should talk about 'he', 'she' or 'they', not 'I' or 'we'.

A successful news report will:

- give a detailed description of an event
- use words and phrases specific to what's being written about
- include all the important facts, missing nothing out
- give a clear explanation of where and why the event happened
- have a headline that relates to the article.

Exercises

Get a copy of *First News*. This is a newspaper written especially for children your age. Go to the *First News* website, www.firstnews.co.uk, and look at past issues. Spend some time reading articles and checking them against the criteria listed above.

Look at the features common to most of the articles: a headline is followed by an opening sentence written in **bold** type, then text in non-bold type. Most articles are accompanied by photographs or pictures.

Why have a headline?

The headline is designed to grab readers' attention. It should be short but give an indication of the article's content.

What purpose does the sentence in bold type serve?

It tells readers what the rest of the article is about, summing it up as informatively as possible.

Newspaper artices are written in columns. Create a page with columns, and space for a headline and a picture.

Look at the diagrams to help you.

 ## Go and do!

- What is happening in your school? Are you preparing for an assembly, visiting the High School, expecting an important visitor, or something else? Make careful notes on what is happening. Think back to the previous unit on making notes. Remember to use 'text speak' when making notes. Ask your friends or a teacher for their views on the event. Write an article on your chosen event. Use the newspaper layout you prepared earlier. The first sentence should be in bold type and briefly sum up the content of the article. Try to include a quote from someone at the centre of the event. Think of a suitable headline and either draw a picture or attach a photograph of the event.

 ## High 5!

In my news articles I:

- write in the third person

- describe the event in detail

- include all the important facts, missing nothing out

- give a clear indication of why and where the event happened

- include a headline.

Check-up tasks

 Help! Keep going! Good to go!

Look at a newspaper with your child. If it is an adult newspaper, choose suitable articles to discuss. Ask your child to point out the common features of the chosen articles and to explain the intention of the headlines, first sentences and pictures.

Breaking news

> ## This section will:
>
> - explain the function of 'breaking news' or 'Stop Press' columns in newspapers
> - help you create breaking news items
> - encourage you to have fun recording your breaking news items using your computer, mobile phone, etc.

News as it happens

Newspapers and news programmes tell us what has been happening in the world around us. We learn about local, national and global events. News items on the TV are placed in order of importance, with the most important coming first. In a newspaper, what the editors consider to be the most important item is placed on the front page. This is known as the headline article. Less important news is placed inside the newspaper.

Sometimes, however, important news happens as a paper is about to go to press or a news programme is about to go on air. It is too late to rearrange the news items or to reprint the paper. In a newspaper this important news is often placed in a column titled 'Stop press'. In other words, the press (the machine that prints the newspaper) is stopped long enough for a short item to be written, and inserted in a small column, detailing important recent news. Live radio and television programmes can, however, react to these important news items in a different way. They will interrupt the agreed order of news items with the words 'news just in' or 'breaking news'.

Breaking news can be anything really important, including:
- the death of an important person
- a major earthquake, erupting volcano, tsunami, hurricane, etc.
- severe local weather warnings
- terrorist attacks.

Top Tips for Parents

- **Glow** is a national intranet for education and is unique to Scotland. All school children in Scotland should have been given Glow log-ons and passwords. However, schools need to give permission for their pupils to access the site outside school. If your child's school has not given this permission ask if this could be done, explaining why. Don't worry if this request is denied. **The Daily What** can still be accessed and the articles read, although your child will not be able to use any of the interactive activities.
- Point out to your child any 'breaking news' or 'stop press' items you hear on the news or read in the papers.
- The following news websites may also be useful but they are not specifically for children. Using a variety of sources is always a good idea though.
  www.bbc.co.uk/news
  www.itv.com/news

Go and do!

You may be familiar with the following website www.dailywhat.org.uk/

This is an online newspaper for schools. It is part of *The Herald* newspaper and can also be accessed through the national site on Glow. If you have a Glow password and have been given permission to use it outside school, log in and you will be able to take part in any of the interactive activities. If you are unable to log in to Glow, ask your teacher if you can be given this permission. It is not necessary, however, to be logged in to Glow to complete the following task.

Like a newspaper, *The Daily What* is divided into pages – World, Politics, Environment, Health, Science & Technology, Entertainment and Sport. Check out each page using the tabs. The most important item of the day is placed at the top of each page with the title 'Top Story'. The less important, but no less interesting, stories are placed below these. Look through them and read the ones that interest you the most.

- Think of an incident or phenomenon that could be considered breaking news.
- Make notes on how you would report this news to the public if you were the news reporter. Remember how you wrote a news item – mention the breaking news in the first sentence, then go on to give more details, for example:
  We interrupt this report to bring you breaking news. A major earthquake has occurred …
- Once you have decided on the item and what you want to say, write it out and practise reading it as if you were really a news reporter. Make changes, if necessary, to your report, then, when you are happy with it, record it using a computer software package such as Audacity, an iPod, a mobile phone, a dictaphone, or a video or digital camera. Listen to the recording. Have another go if you wish to alter or improve anything.

High 5!

- I understand why newspapers have a 'Stop press' column.

- I can write a successful, short breaking news item.

- I can record my item, replay it and make improvements if necessary.

Check-up tasks

Listen to your child's recording. Has he or she managed to record a successful breaking news item?

Write a commentary

This section will:

- explain when commentaries are used
- help you write your own humorous commentaries
- encourage you to record your commentaries using a computer, a mobile phone, etc.
- link commentary-writing to the section on making notes (pages 64–65).

making notes (pages 64–65).

Top Tips for Parents

- Try to get your child to listen to a variety of commentaries, not just sport. Listen to documentaries about famous people in the music business or programmes about wildlife, for example. If your child has a particular interest in something then that is a good place to start.

What are commentaries?

We regularly listen to commentaries, especially if we are keen on sport. Commentaries can be delivered at great speed or at a slower pace. Sometimes they are at a mixture of speeds.

The slower the pace of the event, the slower the commentary. Commentaries delivered at slower paces include:

- royal weddings and state funerals
- cricket matches
- snooker games
- those for some features on television such as animal documentaries and music programmes.

Some events, especially those which are carried out at speed, require the commentary to be very fast. Commentaries such as these include:

- motor racing
- sprint races.

Some events, however, have a mixture of speeds. The event may start slow and finish at speed or the speed may vary throughout the commentary. These types of event include:

- horse racing – the commentary speeds up as the horses near the finish line.

Go and do!

Write and deliver a speedy commentary.

- Imagine your mum, or whoever does the shopping in your house, has won a supermarket sweep. She must turn up at the supermarket along with another winner, where they will be given five minutes to fill their trolleys. The ultimate winner is the person whose filled trolley has the higher value at the end of the five minutes.

- This supermarket sweep is being broadcast on the radio and you are the commentator. You will need to give a very graphic account of what is happening as the commentary is on the radio, not the television. Make notes under the following headings, which will help you when writing the commentary. Remember many supermarkets now sell large and small electrical goods, clothes and garden furniture, etc. Try to make your commentary as humorous as possible.

- **What is each person doing prior to the start?** Are they, for instance stretching, jogging on the spot, standing on a box looking for the best aisle to start in?

- **When the whistle is blown, which aisle does each person head for?**

- **What incidents occur?** E.g. wheel falls off a trolley, trolleys collide, crash into a display which falls over.

- **Anything else?** E.g. little old lady gets in the way, attack each other with shopping bags, can't lift heavy item into trolley.

- **Who wins?**

- Once you have written your commentary, practise reading it. Remember, you will start off quite slowly as you describe what each winner is doing before the start. As the contest begins you will start to get quite excited, gather speed and may even get louder. If you have typed your commentary, print another copy and ask a partner to provide sound effects such as the whistle, clash of trolleys and so on.

- Record your commentary and listen to it. Can you improve it? Have another try if you feel you could do better.

 ## High 5!

- I understand why and when commentaries are used.

- I can write a successful humorous commentary.

- I can record my commentary, listen to the playback and amend my work if necessary.

Check-up tasks

Help!　Keep going!　Good to go!

Listen to the commentary. Has your child injected some humour into it? Did he or she remember to speed up, increase and decrease the volume and vary the expression in his or her voice?

Make it rhyme

This section will:

- encourage you to search the internet for interesting poetry websites
- ask you to check out online rhyming dictionaries
- help you write a good rhyming poem.

Top Tips for Parents

- Encourage your child to read and listen to both traditional and modern poems. Use the internet to help you find a range of poetry to interest your child.
- The following site for children has well-known poets reading and talking about their poems. Allow your child to investigate all the site has to offer. www.poetryarchive.org/childrensarchive/home.do
- This site has a long list of more traditional children's poems, which should broaden your child's understanding of poetry. www.storyit.com/Classics/JustPoems/index.htm
- This site has some fun poems which should encourage the most reluctant poet. www.fizzyfunny fuzzy.com/showpoem.php?poemID=76

Rhyme time

From a very early age we are taught to listen for words that rhyme through hearing nursery rhymes, rhyming stories and rhyming poems. Most young children enjoy simple rhymes and, after hearing a rhyme a few times, will happily join in with the end of lines. You were probably taught to spell as an infant by using rhyme, e.g. words that end with an 'ar' sound – jar, car, far, bar, tar.

Although we can hear words that rhyme, we often find writing a rhyme very difficult. We are so busy trying to find a word that rhymes with a previous one that we forget the poem must also be good. If you do this, the end result can be quite disappointing.

 ## Exercises

The internet is a great place to start learning how to write a rhyming poem. Online rhyming dictionaries can be powerful tools to help you to find rhyming words.

Log on to one of the following:

www.rhymezone.com/

www.poetry4kids.com/modules.php?name=Rhymes

- Think of a word, e.g. 'sister', and type it into the search bar. Note how many rhyming words it produces.
- Try this exercise several times with different words. Some words will produce lots of rhyming words and others very few. When writing a rhyming poem, it is important to remember this fact and try to avoid having to use this type of word as part of the rhyme. The word 'orange', for example, has no rhyming partner. It would be fine to use it in the middle of a line but not at the end where you might want it to rhyme with another word.

Go and do!

Write a rhyming poem. Don't try to be too adventurous to start with. Begin with an easy idea and, as you acquire the skills needed to be successful, start to write more complicated rhymes.

- The following site gives some great ideas on how to start a rhyming poem. It was created by the American poet Kenn Nesbitt.

www.poetry4kids.com/

When you have seen all that the site has to offer, click on the **Poetry Lessons** icon. Here you can read four chapters on how to write a funny poem. Read through each one carefully.

- Leave the website running on your computer so that you can refer to it at any time. Use a word-processing package or a piece of paper to write down a list of ideas you may want to use for your poem. Kenn Nesbitt explains how to do this in Chapter 3.
- Write down words to do with the topic you have chosen. For example, if you are writing about space you may have the words space, Earth, Mars, comet, rocket, Sun, asteroid, etc. Now use an online rhyming dictionary to come up with as many words as possible that rhyme with your chosen words.
- Write a short rhyming poem about your topic. Use the website to help you if you get stuck. Give your poem a title and include your name at the end. Is your poem good enough to submit to Kenn Nesbitt's website in the 'Poem-Writing Contests' section?

High 5!

- I can use the internet to search for children's poetry.
- I have read and understood many different kinds of poems.
- I am able to use internet rhyming dictionaries to help me write a rhyming poem to convey my thoughts and feelings.

Check-up tasks

Read the poems created by your child. How successful are they? Encourage your child to keep trying.

Help! Keep going! Good to go!

Poetry

This section will:

- explain the rules for writing haikus
- explain the importance of syllables in some poetry
- help you create your own haiku and rap
- encourage you to record your rap using a computer, a mobile phone, or other device.

The power of poetry

Poetry comes in many forms and guises. It can rhyme or not rhyme, tell stories and be humorous or serious. Poetry is written for all ages, for both children and adults. The first poems most of us remember are nursery rhymes. Think of *Little Bo Peep*, *Jack and Jill*, *Humpty Dumpty* and *Little Jack Horner*. This is a form of poetry many of us will remember for the rest of our lives.

Haiku

Haiku (pronounced *hi coo*) is a Japanese traditional form of poetry. Haikus have a simple formula:

- each consists of three lines
- the first line has five syllables, the second line seven syllables and the third line five syllables.

Remember

Syllables are the individual sounds, or units, that make up words. They are a vowel by itself or a vowel with consonants. Sometimes the letter 'y' replaces a vowel.

- po – e – try   'poetry' has three syllables.
- in – tro – duc – tion   'introduction' has four syllables.
- rhyme   'rhyme' has one syllable.
- lett – er   'letter' has two syllables.

Haikus seldom rhyme. Look at the following example.

Winter sky is grey.	*Five syllables*
Snow falls softly all around.	*Seven syllables*
Water turns to ice.	*Five syllables*

Rap

Rap is a very popular form of rhyming poetry. Rap is often set to music and used by groups and other artistes. Rap always has a distinctive and regular beat or rhythm. Try clapping your hands or clicking your fingers when speaking rap to help keep the beat. A good rap should read like a chant.

The following is an excerpt from a rap by Wes Magee. You can read the whole rap, and listen to the author reading it, at the following website:

www.poetryarchive.org/childrensarchive/singlePoem.do?poemld=382

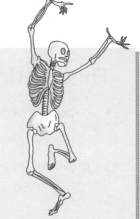

The Boneyard Rap

This is the rhythm of the boneyard rap,
knuckle bones click and hand bones clap,
finger bones flick and thigh bones slap,
when you're doing the rhythm of the boneyard rap.
Wooooooooo!

Wes Magee, *The Boneyard Rap and Other Poems*

Go and do!

- Choose a season or an animal and think about what is special or distinctive about it. Remember the rules for writing haikus. Stick to the three lines and the five-syllable, seven-syllable, five-syllable structure. Write two or three haikus. Choose the one you like the best or the one you feel is most successful, write it neatly using a computer or on a good piece of paper, then illustrate it with colourful pictures or clip art.
- Write your own raps. Remember that they should rhyme and have a rhythm or a beat. Use the rhyming dictionary you can find at the following website if you are having difficulty thinking of rhyming words: www.poetry4kids.com/modules.php?name=Rhymes
- Record yourself reading your raps. It would be fun to ask a friend to read the rap with you.

High 5!

- I can write a successful haiku of three lines with the required syllables. ☐ ☐ ☐

- I can write a rap with rhyming words, using an online rhyming dictionary if necessary. ☐ ☐ ☐

- I can record my work using a computer, a mobile phone, etc. ☐ ☐ ☐

Check-up tasks

Help!   Keep going!   Good to go!

Read the poems written by your child.
- Has he or she fully understood the idea of syllables when writing haikus?   ◯ ◯ ◯
- Help with the beat or rhythm of the rap if necessary.   ◯ ◯ ◯
- Listen to your child reading the poems.   ◯ ◯ ◯

Write and record a play or drama

This section will:

- explain the criteria for writing successful plays and dramas
- encourage you to write and record plays, design costumes and consider sound effects.

What is drama?

A play or drama should be an exciting or emotional piece of writing. It is written to be performed by actors for the enjoyment of an audience.

Like imaginative writing, a play tells a story. Unlike imaginative writing, the story in a play is told completely through dialogue. We learn about our characters and the storyline or plot of the play, not through descriptive prose but by what the characters say and how they say it. When we read a play we are told who speaks and what they say. However, the actors who speak the written lines need to know some other things as well.

- How should they speak their lines – are they angry, happy, sad, whispering, scared, etc?
- Are they speaking directly to another character, to themselves or to the audience?
- Where should they be on the stage?
- When do they enter or exit the stage?
- Do they need to do anything whilst saying their lines? Maybe they are eating, on the phone, playing with a ball or dancing.

What this means is that as well as writing the play or drama, you have to write stage directions.

When we write plays we write the name of the character who is speaking, followed by a colon before writing what he or she says. How they are speaking and other information is written in italics and/or in brackets. This lets the actors know that they do not speak these words.

(Mum sits reading at side of stage. Martin sits with his back to her at a desk on the opposite side.)

Mum (shouting):	Martin! Have you finished your homework?
Martin (muttering):	Not yet mum.
Mum (angry):	You'd better not be playing that computer game again.

Go and do!

Write a play with a difference.

- Look at this list of well-known fairytales.
    - *Little Red Riding Hood*
    - *The Three Little Pigs*
    - *Hansel and Gretel*
- Select one of the fairytales listed or choose your own. Think how you could make it different. Ask yourself 'What if …?'
    - What if the wolf was the good guy and granny was the baddie?
    - What if Hansel and Gretel were really wicked and the witch was a good fairy?
- Write your play on paper or using a computer. Try to make it humorous. Keep the number of actors in your play to a minimum. Having too many characters can be confusing. Remember to include stage directions.
- Think about sound effects (often written as 'sound FX') that would be needed to help make your play more realistic, e.g.
    - a knock on the door
    - a phone ringing
    - water dripping.
- Make a list of the sound FX in your play and incorporate them in the script. Remember, if you are using a computer, to write these in italics.
- Finally, if you have some willing friends or family, act out your play. Give people different parts, rehearse the script and have fun.
- If you have access to a video camera, set it up on a tripod or ask someone to operate it for you. Record your play to watch later.

High 5!

- I can successfully write a play with stage directions and sound effects. ☐ ☐ ☐
- I have taken part in the reading of a play script and have used my voice to portray a character. ☐ ☐ ☐

Check-up tasks

How well written was your child's play? Did it include coherent dialogue and sufficient stage directions?

Help!   Keep going!   Good to go!

◯   ◯   ◯

Scots language

> ## This section will:
>
> - explain the origins of the Scots language
> - give some Scots words with their English equivalents
> - encourage you to start a Scots dictionary.

Where does Scots come from?

Scots owes its origins to the many tribes and invaders that have made Scotland home during its rich and colourful history. Many words in common usage now can be traced to the Celts, the Romans, the Vikings from Denmark and Norway, the Angles from Germany and the French, to name a few. Here are some examples of words in Scots that have come from other languages.

- *Hus* (pronounced hoos) is Danish for house.
- *Barn* is Norwegian for child.
- *Kuh* (pronounced coo) is German for cow.
- The Scots word *ashet*, meaning a large plate, comes from the French '*une assiette*', meaning 'a plate'.

There are several dialects of Scots. These include Ayrshire, Doric, Shetland and Glaswegian. Words that are used regularly in some parts of Scotland may have fallen out of favour in others.

Living in Scotland we use and hear Scots words wherever we go. Many of us speak Scots in the home and with school pals. We hear it in the supermarket, at the bus stop and in the playground. As we are so used to listening and speaking Scots, we are not always aware of it and we can easily go between English and Scots depending on who we are talking to. English is very often used in the classroom and when speaking to non-Scottish people. It is used when being interviewed for jobs. When we are relaxing with family or friends we speak Scots.

Top Tips for Parents

- For many years the Scots language was considered slang and children were encouraged not to speak it. In recent years, however, Scots has been recognised, by both the Scottish and UK governments, as a distinct language, which should be embraced in its own right. It should not be confused with Gaelic.
- Scots should not be considered as slang, although there are slang words in Scots!
- Libraries and bookshops should have children's books written in Scots. Encourage your child to read some of these, both for pleasure and information.
- *Collins Gem Scots Dictionary* can be bought in most good bookshops and on the internet. It is an ideal source of Scottish words and phrases suitable for both children and adults.
- Use the internet to find more Scots words and their meanings. However, be aware that some sites are not moderated and may contain words and phrases unsuitable for your child, so check first. For Scots poems try: www.scotsindependent. org/features/scots/ children.htm

Scots words in common usage include:

crabbit – bad-tempered

aye – yes

naw – no

lugs – ears

quine (Doric – sometimes spelt *quean*) – girl

loon (Doric) – lad

hirple – limp

scunnered – fed up

drookit – soaked or drenched

wean (Glasgow), *bairn* – baby or small child

stank (Glasgow) – drain

syver (some rural areas around Glasgow) – drain

brander (Doric) – drain

fit like (Doric) – How are you?

wee – small

oxter – armpit

crabbit!

 ## Exercises

Rewrite the following in English – use an internet search engine if you get stuck.

- 'Hey Maw, canna huv a piece an jam?'
- The rain is stottin doon.
- Ma semmit was maukit so ma mither washed it.
- The midden was fair mingin.
- The polis kent whar baith prisoners whar.

Go and do!

- Start a Scots/English dictionary. To do this, think of all the Scots words you know. Ask a family member or a friend when you're unsure whether a word is Scots or not. Write the words down alphabetically with their meanings in English next to them. Listen to Scottish programmes and plays on television and the radio, read some Scottish books, search the internet – how many Scots words can you come up with? Why not illustrate your dictionary with pictures and, like a standard dictionary, give the origins of the words, their pronunciation and parts of speech. You could also use the words in sentences to illustrate their meanings.

- Study the list of Scots words in the box below. On a piece of paper draw two columns and give them the headings: creatures, other. Place each word in the box in the correct column along with its meaning in English. Use the internet or a good Scots dictionary to help if you're stuck. Why not add any new words to your own Scots dictionary!

bubblyjock	clocker	joukin	selkie	brock
muckle	poke	yowe	midden	speug
sonsie	partan	lum	bide	simmit
fankle	pech	hurcheon	puggy	gallus
maukin	mawkit	braw	paddock	corby
stooshie	stuckie	stoorie	hackit	clarty

- You should have quite a list of Scots words and their meanings now. Can you draw cartoon type pictures to illustrate some of them? Write what they are in Scots. Look at the following examples.

A bairn wi a gird 'n cleek

A speug

- Create and play a pelmanism game, (sometimes called pairs) with a friend.
  - You need approximately thirty pieces of paper or card.
  - Write the Scots words on half the pieces (one word per piece – use the words from your Scots dictionaries) and their English equivalents on the other half.
  - Mix them up and spread them across the table top or floor.
  - Turn two cards over. If you get a matching pair you win the set.

- If the words do not match turn the cards back over again.
- Keep going until all the cards are used.
- The person with the most pairs wins.

- Visit the library or local bookshop. There are many books written in Scots specifically for youngsters. Borrow or buy some books. Use them to add words to your dictionary as well as to enjoy their content. Try looking for books that have rewritten common fairytales in Scots. You can also find the Bible written in Scots! Reading these well-known stories helps us to understand the words used as well as providing us with great entertainment. Perhaps you and your friends could act some of these stories out.

 ## High 5!

- I have extended my knowledge of Scots words and can use them correctly.

☐ ☐ ☐

- I have read and understood some Scots poems and stories.

☐ ☐ ☐

- I can use Scots language in my writing.

☐ ☐ ☐

- I am able to use the internet and reference books to look up unknown Scots words to discover their derivations and meanings.

☐ ☐ ☐

Check-up tasks

Help!   Keep going!   Good to go!

- Look through the Scots dictionary your child has compiled or use the words from the pelmanism game. Choose some words at random and ask him/her some questions. E.g. 'What is a rammy?', 'What is the Scots word for a small paper bag?'

○   ○   ○

- Look at a simple fairytale. Could your child translate a small passage from it into Scots?

○   ○   ○

- If you have been able to buy or borrow a book of fairytales in Scots, can your child read and understand it?

○   ○   ○

Genre and style

> ## This section will:
>
> - give the definition of 'genre'
> - encourage you to consider your preferred genre of books
> - help you think about the style a writer uses.

What is a genre?

Collins Online English Dictionary gives the definition of 'genre' as:

> **Genre**
>
> a kind or type of literary, musical or artistic work

Musical genres include jazz, rap, rock, country or opera.

Artistic genres include landscape, abstract, seascape, oil or watercolour.

We are going to concentrate, however, on **literary genres**. There are many genres in this category, including horror, science fiction, autobiography, biography, mystery, adventure, instruction, humour, history, poetry, fantasy, romance, business, sport, gardening, travel, science, information, cookery and picture books. Look at the different sections in the library or local bookshop. The books are separated by genre. The genre is always used as a title for the section where you find the books.

Every author has a style of writing that is unique to them. You will have a favourite author or authors. He or she will be your favourite because you like what they write about (genre) and you like how they write (style). Perhaps his or her style captures your imagination and excites your feelings and senses. Perhaps you like the author's choice of words and the way he or she uses them to describe scenes, events and characters.

Go and do!

- Look around your home. Make lists of the books you see, placing all the books in a similar genre in the same list. Don't just concentrate on your own books but look at those belonging to the rest of your family – brother, sister, parents or carers.

- Read the following text excerpt. Discuss the genre and style with a partner, and then either write a few more sentences to continue the story, or work with your partner and tell one another what you think happens next. Remember:
  - Keep the characters the same.
  - Stay within the genre.
  - Try to keep the style of writing similar to the author's.
  - If speech is used, keep the style, including humour, fear etc. the same.

He was not alone. Oliver knew that immediately. He propped himself up on his freezing elbows and peered into the night. Yes! There at the end of his bed, he made out a figure both black and silvery in the midnight gloom. A swirling mist of long hair rose and fell around it. And the face in the middle of that hair was like a sort of everlasting firework – exploding, but exploding silently, putting itself together once more, staring around the world and then exploding all over again.

'Who are you?' Oliver asked, as well as he could between his tap-dancing teeth.

'I am a ghost,' said the ghost. 'I am sick of haunting my own house next door. There's never anyone there to terrify, so I have come to terrify you.'

'You won't t-t-t-terrify me,' chattered Oliver. 'I'm not t-t-t-terrifyable.'

But this was not quite true.

The Shadow Thief, Margaret Mahy, from a book of short stories, *Kids' Night In*

 High 5!

- I understand the meaning of the word 'genre'.
- I can categorise books by genre.
- I can consider a writer's style and successfully re-create it.

Check–up tasks

Ask your child to find books in the house that illustrate a selection of genres, e.g. cookery, information, travel, mystery, humour and autobiography.

Help!　Keep going!　Good to go!

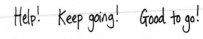

Stories/give a talk

This section will:

- explain the purpose of myths, legends and traditional stories
- encourage you to select a topic to research
- give hints and tips on how to deliver a talk.

The importance of stories

There are myths, legends and traditional tales told in every culture throughout the world. They are stories from long ago that have been passed down through the generations. Initially they would have been passed through word of mouth, stories told around fires at night entertaining both children and adults. Eventually these stories were written down for the next generation to read, listen to and enjoy.

A **myth** is a story that has been told to try to explain the way things are, why things happen and the relationships between gods and humans. It is highly unlikely that the events depicted in myths could ever be possible. Many well-known myths originate from Ancient Rome and Greece, e.g. 'King Midas', and 'Pandora's Box'.

A **legend** is a traditional story based on truth. However, bits have been added to it to make it a more exciting story, like 'The Legends of King Arthur'.

A **traditional story** is just that – a story which has been told for many generations. The origins often may have been forgotten but we still enjoy listening to such stories. These include 'Cinderella' and 'The Billy Goats Gruff'.

Go and do!

Using your research skills, you are going to research and give a short talk on a traditional tale, a myth or a legend. Choose from myths, legends or traditional tales.

Myths	Legends	Traditional tales
• Jason and the Argonauts	• Sawney Bean	• Robin Hood
• Beowulf	• Romulus and Remus	• Sinbad
• Hercules	• The Wooden Horse of Troy	• The Kelpie

Spend some time researching a little about each of the options before making a final choice. Once you have decided what to talk about you will need to research your chosen topic thoroughly.

- Use the internet, visit your local library or use your own reference books. It is best to use more than one source of information. Don't forget to make a note of each book or website you use.
- Take plenty of notes, keeping every detail in the correct order.
- Decide how you are going to give your talk. Will you have handwritten notes in front of you? Would you prefer to use a PowerPoint display or a series of pictures for which you will provide the commentary?
- Looking down at your paper or turning your back on your audience when talking will muffle your voice and lacks spontaneity. Hold your head up when talking; vary the tone of your voice and, above all, look directly at your audience. If talking to more than one person, look at each one in turn.
- Giving a talk can be extremely nerve-racking. It is essential, however, that you take a deep breath, and stand with your shoulders back and your head held high. Believe that this is something you can do. Learning how to control your nerves will stand you in good stead for the future.

High 5!

- I can select a topic to research, make notes and deliver my findings to others as a talk. ☐ ☐ ☐

- I can give a talk using a clear voice, expression and gesture. ☐ ☐ ☐

Check-up tasks

Help!   Keep going!   Good to go!

Listen carefully to your child's talk. Besides checking how well he or she has researched and prepared the chosen subject, assess the following:

- How confident does he or she appear to be?
- Does he or she speak clearly without reading constantly from their notes?
- Does he or she maintain eye contact with their audience?

When the talk is finished, ask one or two questions about the subject.

Be positive! Offer praise for the things done well and give helpful hints on how to improve next time.

Fact or opinion?

> ## This section will:
>
> - explain the difference between fact and opinion
> - link facts and opinions to persuade or argue? (pages 92–93).

What's the difference?

A **fact** is the truth. It is something we cannot argue against or doubt. In Law-courts facts are used as evidence.

An **opinion** is a point of view. It is a belief held by one person or by a group of people. An opinion is not necessarily true.

Some people use their opinions to influence how we think and behave. It is important, therefore, when reading articles on the internet, in magazines or books or when listening to someone speak, that we are able to differentiate between facts and opinions. In other words, not everything we read, or hear, is true.

FACT Many people enjoy watching football.   **OPINION** All people enjoy watching football.

Exercises

Read the following extracts.

Children in Victorian times lived very different lives from yours today. In many ways, they were treated like little adults. Unless they came from a rich family, they had to go out to work to earn money. But it was not work like today's holiday jobs or paper rounds. It meant working long hours six days a week, doing horrible jobs that were boring or dangerous, or both!

Poor families lived in small, crowded houses built in back-to-back rows. Many had only two rooms. They were dirty and dark inside, as the windows were often broken and stuffed with rags to keep out the cold. Often children had to share a room, and even a bed, with their parents.

Most children started work in coal mines at the age of eight or nine. Some worked the pumps to keep water out of the tunnels and they often had to stand with their feet in cold water for eight hours a day. In Scotland, girls had to carry baskets of coal up the ladders beside the pit shafts, even though their loads could weigh up to 150 kilograms.

Jillian Powell, *Hard Times: Growing up in the Victorian Age*

Now read the following statements. Who is stating facts and who is voicing opinions? Write your choice beside each child's name.

Josh		Marcia	
1	Poor Victorian children enjoyed working.	1	Children today do not have the same lives as children living in the Victorian era.
2	All jobs done by Victorian children were boring.	2	There were very few rooms in the homes of poor people.
3	Poor Victorians were lazy and didn't repair their homes.	3	Many poor Victorians could only afford one bed.
4	In the coal mines the only job children did was to work the pumps.	4	In Scotland girls carried heavy baskets of coal up ladders.

 Go and do!

- Copy the table below onto a piece of paper.

FACT	OPINION

- Now read a newspaper. Find at least five facts and at least five opinions in the paper and add them to the correct columns in the table. Ask a partner if he or she agrees with your choice. Explain why you made these choices.

 High 5!

- I can differentiate between fact and opinion. ☐ ☐ ☐

- I realise some people will try to influence me by stating their opinions and not facts. ☐ ☐ ☐

- I understand that not everything I read or hear is true. ☐ ☐ ☐

Check-up tasks

Help!   Keep going!   Good to go!

Ask your child to explain the difference between fact and opinion. Below are two facts and two opinions. Can your child say which is which?

1 The Earth orbits the Sun. ◯ ◯ ◯

2 *Harry Potter and the Philosopher's Stone* is a good book and a good film. ◯ ◯ ◯

Persuade or argue?

This section will:

- explain what persuasion is
- give reasons why you should be aware of fact and opinion in arguments
- make you aware of why it is important to recognise bias in both spoken and written work
- encourage you to take part in a debate.

The difference between persuasion and argument

Persu`hen we try to convince people that what we are thinking, saying or doing is correct. They may disagree with us to start with but, hopefully, using persuasion, we can convince them otherwise.

I'm sure you have had arguments with parents, siblings or friends. An argument is when we disagree with someone over an opinion we hold. They think one thing and we think another.

There are other types of arguments, however. Some arguments are planned. Two or more people put forward opposite views and try to persuade us that their views are the correct ones. These arguments are often referred to as debates. They are held so that we can formulate opinions for ourselves on what we believe or what we want to do. These arguments are often held in large halls or broadcast on the television or radio, to maximise the number of people who can hear them. Politicians use this form of persuasion all the time. Local councillors and MPs hold this type of discussion when they want us to vote for or against something. Politicians, especially the leaders of the main political parties, hold live debates on television before major elections. Each politician wants us to vote for his or her party and uses debates to try to persuade us that his or her political view is the right one.

Arguments and debates do not have to be spoken. Many are written down and published in book form. We can buy these, if we wish, in bookshops or borrow them from the library. Such a book, of course, usually has only one point of view – the author's – so we need to be aware of what is fact and what is opinion, and use the information in the book to formulate our own opinions. Having a strong opinion on something and trying to persuade others to share your opinion is often referred to as being biased. We need to be able to recognise bias when we hear it or read it, and strive not to be influenced by it.

Many schools have debating clubs or societies for pupils. These are designed to teach us how to persuade and argue effectively. If you are in a debating club you may be asked to argue for something you don't believe in. This doesn't matter. The intention is that you learn how to put forward a point of view by researching the topic being debated, in particular the view you have been asked to argue for, and put together a good argument to prove your case. The audience-members will listen to both sides of the argument and then vote for the one they prefer. The winner is the person who can persuade the most people that their view is the best. You could make a list of arguments to help you organise your thoughts.

 ## Go and do!

- If possible, work with a partner. Choose a subject that matters to you and your friends. Decide who will argue for the motion and who will argue against it. Research, if necessary, and make notes on the side you are arguing for. Now write your argument down. You should:
  - Include an introduction – this should start with a rhetorical question. A rhetorical question is one that is asked purely for effect. It is designed to make a statement rather than be answered, e.g. in a debate about whether we should be asked to wear school uniforms a candidate might start his argument with the rhetorical question, 'School uniforms – why should we be made to wear them?'
  - Say what your opinions are on the subject.
  - Give details or evidence to support your opinions – each paragraph should state a reason and be justified. (Justified means give reasons why you think this way.)
  - Finish with a closing statement – this should link with the opinion you made at the beginning.

 ## High 5!

- I can identify fact and opinion. ☐ ☐ ☐

- I know when someone is trying to change my opinion. ☐ ☐ ☐

- I am aware of bias and know when someone is trying to influence me. ☐ ☐ ☐

- I can present an argument in a debate, providing evidence to support my opinion. ☐ ☐ ☐

Check-up tasks

How good was your child's argument? Was he or she able to put forward views effectively and forcibly without becoming angry?

Help!   Keep going!   Good to go!
◯   ◯   ◯

Functional letter writing

This section will:

- explain how to write a formal letter to someone you don't know
- give the accepted criteria for a functional letter.

What is a functional letter?

Functional letters are written for a purpose. It may be a letter of complaint, invitation or thanks. It can be written asking for advice, or requesting information. Functional letters are usually written to people we have never met so it is very important that we follow the rules of letter writing.

A successful functional letter will:

- include the conventions of letter writing, e.g. address, greeting and sign-off
- be written in a style that is appropriate to the intended reader
- explain clearly and accurately why you are writing
- be well organised and clearly presented.

A completed letter should have:

- your address written at the top of the letter
- the date written below the address
- a suitable greeting – *'Dear Sir or Madam'* if you don't know the person's name
- an opening sentence explaining your reason for writing
- paragraphs – not necessarily indented but marked by leaving a line space between the end of one and the beginning of the next.
- separate paragraphs for each argument (*see Persuade or argue?* on pages 92–93)
- a concluding paragraph that repeats the reason you have written the letter
- a formal ending, using the words *'Yours sincerely'* if you have used the person's name in the greeting or *'Yours faithfully'* if your greeting was *'Dear Sir or Madam'*
- your name, including surname, at the end.

Look at the example of a formal letter below.

3 North Street

Bridgetown

Fife K 16 8 W

17th February 2011

Dear Sir or Madam,

I am writing to complain about the state of the ground behind my house. People have been using it to dump unwanted household rubbish such as fridges, bicycles and sofas. As well as being an eyesore, we are worried for the children who play on the ground. There is a lot of broken glass and dangerous pieces of metal. We have even seen rats late at night! Please could you send some workers with a truck to clean it up.

My friends and I were thinking that if all the rubbish were removed, then the ground could be turned into a great park as we have nowhere safe to play.

Yours faithfully,

Dawn Farmer

Remember:

- Always be polite.
- State the reason for your letter.
- Give evidence to support your complaint or to clarify the points you make.

 ## Go and do!

- Write a letter to a famous person – such as a sports personality, pop star or author, asking them to visit your school. Explain why you would like them to visit and the day and time that would suit you best. You should state the name of your school as well as telling a little about yourself, such as your age and why you admire the person.

 ## High 5!

When writing a functional letter I remember to:

- use the conventions of letter writing

- write in a style suitable for the intended reader

- explain why I am writing.

☐ ☐ ☐
☐ ☐ ☐
☐ ☐ ☐

Check-up tasks

Read the letters written by your child. Do they include all the necessary criteria as stated above? Has your child remained polite throughout the letter, mentioned all the important points in the correct order and remembered to write his or her name at the end?

'Look, Say, Cover, Write, Check' method (from page 17)

This method is one useful way of learning how to spell words correctly, but it's not the only one! Try as many different methods as you need to until you find the right ones for you.

First, get a list of words that you have problems spelling.

Look

Look at the word closely. While you look at it, try to figure out which bits of the word will be easy to spell and which parts will need more work.

Say

Now say the word out loud. Saying a word out loud often helps you to find parts of the word that will be tricky to spell.

Cover

Now cover up the word on the page (or on the screen if you're using a computer) so you can't see it.

Write

Write the word down.

Check

Finally, uncover the word and check to see how you've done. Don't worry if you don't get it right on your first attempt. Just keep trying!

There are also websites with the 'Look, Say, Cover, Write, Check' method so you can try online too. One site is at www.amblesideprimary.com/ambleweb/lookcover/lookcover.html

Answers for Make Notes exercise, page 65

Window was broken

Chair knocked over

Cash stolen from safe with old-style dial

Papers lying over the floor and table